Beyond the stable state

Beyond
the
Stable State

DONALD A. SCHON

Random House New York

HN
18
S37
1971

ISBN: 0-394-47293-4
Library of Congress Catalog Card Number: 73-159392

Acknowledgment is extended to Cambridge University Press for
permission to quote from *On Growth And Form*, by
D'Arcy Thompson, edited by J. T. Bonner.

Manufactured in the United States of America

9   8   7   6   5   4   3   2

First American Edition

◆ Contents
◆
◆

◆ Preface

This book was in the making from 1966 to 1970, four years peculiarly conducive to reflection about the Stable State, its loss, and what may lie beyond it.

During this period, I gained a great deal from several individuals and organizations. Projects undertaken with colleagues at OSTI (Organization for Social and Technical Innovation, Inc.) gave me much of the material for the book. My students at MIT's Department of Urban Studies and Planning stimulated a number of ideas and caused me to discard many more. In 1970 the BBC invited me to give the Reith Lectures, an experience which forced me to compress and, I hope, clarify the central arguments of the book. Although I have noted in the text borrowings from the thought of the late Dr Raymond M. Hainer, these convey only a small part of my great indebtedness to him. Finally, I am grateful to Harvard's Program on Technology and Society for their support of my work from 1966 to 1968.

Parts of the book have been published before: Chapter 1, in somewhat different form, was one of a collection of essays brought together in *Transcendence* (Herbert W. Richardson and Donald R. Cutler, eds, Beacon Press, Boston, 1969); versions of Chapters 3 and 4 were published in *Innovation* (No. 6, 1969); parts of Chapter 5 were originally prepared for publication by the Commission on the Year 2000; and passages on blindness were drawn from an article, 'The Blindness System', in *The Public Interest* (No. 18, Winter 1970).

January 1971

1 The loss of the stable state

I have believed for as long as I can remember in an afterlife within my own life—a calm, stable state to be reached after a time of troubles. When I was a child, that afterlife was Being Grown Up. As I have grown older, its content has become more nebulous, but the image of it stubbornly persists.

The afterlife-within-my-life is a form of belief in what I would like to call the Stable State.[1] Belief in the stable state is belief in the unchangeability, the constancy of central aspects of our lives, or belief that we can attain such a constancy. Belief in the stable state is strong and deep in us. We institutionalize it in every social domain. We do this in spite of our talk about change, our apparent acceptance of change and our approval of dynamism. Language about change is for the most part talk about very small change, trivial in relation to a massive unquestioned stability; it appears formidable to its proponents only by the peculiar optic that leads a potato chip company to see a larger bag of potato chips as a new product. Moreover, talk about change is as often as not a substitute for engaging in it.

Belief in the stable state is pervasive:

◆ We believe in the stability of major elements of our own identity such as our occupation or profession. 'I am a chemist,' 'I am a college professor,' 'I am a doctor,' 'I am a cook.' We make such judgments not as tentative findings subject to change but as assertions about enduring aspects of the self. To be unable to make them, or to be ambiguous about them, is a matter for some embarrassment.

◆ Similarly, we believe in the stability of our own regional identity ('I come from Nebraska,' 'I am a Londoner') and of our family backgrounds ('I am a Jones.')

◆ We believe in the stability of the organizations and institutions in which we work ('I work for General Electric') and in the stability of our status or roles within these organizations ('I am financial director') and in the stability of the ideology associated with them ('At Harvard, we respect individual scholarship,' 'At the Lighthouse for the Blind, our concern is with human beings, not with numbers.')

◆ We believe in the stability of intellectual subject matters or disciplines ('My field is physics,' 'I am studying early American history.')

◆ We believe in the stability of certain values—for example, those associated with freedom, work, satisfaction, justice, peace, and the Technological Program, which has aimed since the eighteenth century at a kind of earthly afterlife through technological progress.

Our belief in these various stable states is not always explicit. The General Electric Company has no claim to unquestioned stability, but members of it take its stability for granted. For them the issue is simply not likely to arise, and they accept an unexamined 'as if' stability, a stability for all practical purposes.

Belief in the stable state is central because it is a bulwark against the threat of uncertainty. Given the reality of change, we can maintain belief in the stable state only through tactics of which we are largely unaware. Consequently, our responses to attack on the stable state have been responses of desperation, largely destructive. Our need is to develop institutional structures, ways of knowing, and an ethic, for the process of change itself.

In order to explore this line of argument, we must ask,

What is the function of our belief in the stable state?
How do we maintain it?
What is the nature of the threat to it?
What are the options for response to its loss?

The function of belief in the stable state

Belief in the stable state serves primarily to protect us from apprehension of the threats inherent in change. Belief in stability is a means of maintaining stability, or at any rate the illusion of it. The more radical the prospective change, the more vigorous the defense—the more urgent the commitment to the stable state.

Crises in our lives center around periods of change or transition in which urgent questions of identity are raised. The transition from infancy to the period in which the child learns to say 'I', the beginning of school, puberty, entry into work, marriage, menopause and climacteric, retirement—these are all periods of tension and testing, more or less traumatic. Entry into and release from the army, widowhood, the 'decompression' attendant on return from public life—these are less universal transitions characterized by uneasiness or disruption.

Unexpected instability may be even more disturbing—the marriage that refuses to 'settle down'; change of career; the experience of a woman abandoned by her children; a young man, past college, still unsure of what he wants to do; a mature man, still plagued by the questions of his adolescence. In these situations, the pain of the instability is magnified by the feeling that 'I am not supposed to be experiencing this now.'

These are all experiences in which central elements of the self come into question. They provoke a transformation of the system of the self in which a new zone of stability can be attained only by passing through a zone of instability.

Comparable patterns hold for social systems, for organizations and institutions. These, too, run into zones of crisis and instability:

◆ The business firm, imbued with the tradition of reverence for the founder and all he stood for, forced by shifts in the market and in competition to call into question its theory of operations and its definition of itself as a business.

◆ The social welfare agency whose traditional clientele has gradually disappeared, leaving an institution without a function.

The crisis forces vital elements of the system to change. The change threatens disruption of the stable state whose achievement and maintenance has been central to the existence of the organization.

Social and technological systems interlock. An apparently innocuous change in technology may emerge as a serious threat to an organization because it would force it to transform its theory and structure. Technological, theoretical and social systems exist as aspects of one another; change in one provokes change in the others. And change in organizations has its impact on the person, because beliefs, values and the sense of self have their being in social systems.

In all of these domains of experience, transforming the system means passing through zones of uncertainty. I do not mean risk, the probability of some future event occurring, but the situation of being at sea, of being lost, of confronting more information than you can handle.

The situations of crisis are the ones that provoke

uncertainty. The most threatening changes are the ones that would plunge the system into uncertainty.

◆ I come to be truly confused over the behavior of someone who, until now, has been close to me. His act appears hostile, but may be quite different. How am I to discover? How shall I respond to him?

◆ A psychotherapist who has been working with a patient suddenly finds himself confronted with behavior that belies the hypothesis, the way of seeing the patient, with which he has been working —and there is, as yet, no alternative hypothesis in sight.

◆ A business firm begins to perceive that its product and its marketing policy are inadequate to the demands of the market. The market does not respond to the firm's tested strategies of recovery.

◆ A scientist, committed to a cherished hypothesis, encounters data which do not fit—and which present no clear alternative pattern.

◆ A scientific community—such as the community of physicists in the early years of this century, or the community of nuclear physicists in the last decade —find an entire conceptual framework inadequate to the data presented by a program of experiments which cannot be discredited or abandoned.

In these situations there is not a lack of information. There is not an 'information gap'. There is an information overload, too many signals, more than can be accounted for; and there is as yet no theory in terms of which new information can be sought or new experiments undertaken. 'Uncertainty' is a way of talking about the situation in which no plausible theory has emerged.

For this reason pragmatism[2] is no response. We cannot, in these situations, say 'Let us get the data,' 'Let us experiment,' 'Let us test,' for there is as yet nothing to test. Out of the uncertainty, out of the experience of a bewildering array of information, new hypotheses must emerge—and from them, mandates for gathering data, testing, experiment, can be derived. But in the first instance they do not as yet exist, and until they exist the method of pragmatism cannot be applied. The period of uncertainty must be traversed *in order that* pragmatism may become an appropriate response.

The feeling of uncertainty is anguish. The depth of anguish increases as the threatening changes strike at more central regions of the self. In the last analysis, the degree of threat presented by a change depends on its connection to self-identity.[3] Against all of this we have erected our belief in the stable state.

Tactics for maintenance of belief in the stable state

It is not only in our own time that belief in the stable state has come under attack. Whether we are concerned with perception, personal experience, or the life of organizations and communities, the norm has been flux and variety. Surprises are constantly occurring. In American experience, for example, we seem always to have been in process of change and to have believed in the value of change, and we seem never to have had a national stable state. What is curious is not that we are forced at intervals to abandon some stable state, but that we manage to maintain belief in it in the first place.

The process by which we do so is not passive or inertial but an active and more or less systematic resistance which employs a variety of strategies:

◆ We are selectively inattentive to the data that would upset our current ways of looking at things. It is characteristic of every discovery, in whatever domain, that we are astonished at not having seen it earlier.

◆ We manage a kind of internal economy in which changes in one domain find compensatory stability in others. The private lives of inventors, innovators, artists and discoverers tend to be regular to the point of dull routine.

◆ We undertake a continuous and active program to maintain the system in which we are involved—whether it is the system of the firm, the family, or the self. We keep it in being in the sort of way that a living organism preserves itself by homeostasis. This often takes the form of hostile resistance, overt or underground, to whatever threatens to break up the stable system. Where we cannot help but perceive the change, we strive actively to contain or suppress it. Instances are to be found in the patient's resistance to psychotherapy, the neighborhood's expulsion of troublesome outsiders, the business firm's elaboration of systems to control innovations, the governmental bureaucracies' magnificent semi-conscious system for the long-term wearing down of agents of change.

The effort spent in all of these manoeuvres may be as unconscious as the effort of keeping balance in a small boat.

The nature of the threat to the stable state

In our own time the attack on the stable state has passed beyond what our strategies of resistance can contain. Throughout our society we are experiencing the actual or threatened dissolution of stable organizations and institutions, anchors for personal identity and systems of values. Most important, the stable state itself is becoming less real.

During the last thirty years or so, the United States has experienced three distinct but interacting currents of social change.

◆   A growing awareness and intolerance of the imbalance in our society between the production of
consumer goods, to which the major thrust of the
economy has been devoted, and the critical public
systems such as transportation, housing, education,
and waste disposal, which have taken a poor second
place.

Even though public problems have not necessarily been more severe in the last ten years than in
the last fifty, a rising intolerance of this imbalance
has pervaded recent presidential administrations.
The warcry of awareness came in 1957 with the
publication of John Kenneth Galbraith's book *The
Affluent Society*.

◆   A growing dissatisfaction with the relatively powerless position in American society of many minorities—not only racial (although the demand for de-
colonization of black society in America has been
by far the most visible) but more broadly, the poor,
rural families, the aged, the sick, prisoners, the
mentally ill.

It is as though we were now experiencing, across
the board, a demand that the balance of power
should be righted. This is not merely a demand for
'our share' (as in the programs of the New and Fair
Deals). It includes demands for participation, decentralization, local control, autonomy, that in
recent years have taken on revolutionary propor-
tions.

◆   A growing disenchantment, expressed most vigor-
ously by the young, with the goals and values of
Social Progress, as these have remained relatively
intact since the eighteenth century.

Instead, there is an impetus toward what
Kenneth Keniston has called the New Revolution
—a revolution against economic materialism, uni-

formity, institutional rigidity, centralization, and toward a way of life signaled by terms like participation, openness, and a new ethic of human relationships. The New Revolution shows itself at the moment most intensely in the war of generations and in the refusal of many of the young to be bound by the constraints of established authority.

These are highly visible and broadly recognized, though little understood and inadequately distinguished from one another.

It is usually less broadly recognized that what holds at the most general level of the society holds also for the separate institutions within it. Currents of change roll through every domain of society, shaking the stable state. *No established institution in our society now perceives itself as adequate to the challenges that face it*. Institutions formed in the late years of the nineteenth and early years of the twentieth centuries find themselves threatened by complex changes now underway. In some instances, the very success of their adaptation to the period before World War II, or even to the forties and fifties, makes them inadequate now. There is nothing parochial about this phenomenon. It cuts right through society.

The American Labor Movement suffers from what the more articulate of its leaders are calling 'a failure of success'. Its achievement of the goals of the thirties, which gave Labor its vitality, has left it with a sickening feeling of becoming, not a vital force for social change, but another bureaucratic institution. Labor leaders complain, 'We are becoming middle class.' The young men coming up in the organization seem to the older leaders like young men rising in any bureaucracy; they could be members of middle management in business or the civil service.

A leader like Walter Reuther asked what new missions are appropriate to Labor? What will sustain its sense of mission and vitality? The invention of the concept of 'community union', an attempted response to this uncertainty, is still a vague and unsatisfactory image.

The Federal Government is now under severe attack for its inability to bring resources to bear, quickly and effectively, on such problems as the poor, the decay of the cities, the inadequacy of public education, the inequity of health care. What is new about these problems is not awareness of them, but the level of public intolerance for their continued existence.

One could say, in broad terms, that the government has been seeking to come to grips with these problems through bureaucracies which are memorials to old problems; and to avoid, in the process, creating new bureaucracies which will in turn impede flexible response to still newer problems. There is a sense of the need to invent new roles for the Federal Government in relation to the private sector and to state and local government. Earlier notions of the proper relation between public and private sectors have been eroded by a growing sense of the urgency of public sector problems. And the 1930s view of the proper relation between federal and local government suffers from demands for local autonomy and decentralization, and from the obvious failure of large Federal bureaucracies in providing public services.

The church, in its various denominational guises, finds itself forced to question both its role in society and its organization for carrying out that role. There are, on the one hand, pressures for ecumenism and, on the other, pressures for the same sort of local autonomy that individual neighborhoods and local governments are demanding. There is an urgent demand for moral wisdom which internal conflicts have made it difficult for the church to meet. Parochial sects have tended to dissolve in the face of the media-borne inroads of secular society, while more cosmopolitan religions seem diluted to the point of having little to offer. Many churchmen feel impelled to engage in the battles about poverty, race and the cities; but to the extent that they do so, they tend to estrange themselves from the church.

There is a general disposition to question and to attack the archaic bureaucracy of church organization. But attempts at reform run up against the fear that further liberalization will result in throwing out the baby with the bath water. Disaffection, indifference and open revolt threaten an establishment already troubled over the viability of its traditional intellectual heritage and its spiritual mission. Are these events to be seen as signs of decay or as intimations of new vitality?

Church groups in several denominations ask questions identical to those raised in organizations of business, government and public service: How can we define our appropriate role? How do we work our way into our future? How can we both plan for and induce change? How can we overcome our own resistance to change?

Universities have found themselves under conflicting pressures. Government urges them to assume new national and regional roles for which they are ill-prepared and with which their traditional ideals of scholarship and liberal education conflict. Students press for redistribution of power and for education more relevant to the world outside. The university is set conflicting goals, in preparing students for particular vocations, keeping its own financial autonomy and responding to growing demands for higher education. The functions of education and the role of the university in our society seem hopelessly confused.

This inventory of threatened institutions, each in the grip of an instability imperfectly understood, could be extended in depth and breadth. Enough has been said, perhaps, to show that we are experiencing a general rather than an isolated or peripheral phenomenon.

The threat to the stability of established institutions carries with it a threat to the stability of the theory and ideology associated with them. Institutions like the labor movement, the university, the church, the social welfare agencies, carry with them bodies of theory which constitute ways of looking at the world, and ideologies that govern stance and action. When one of these institutions becomes unstable, its theory and ideology are threatened, and the anchors for identity which they provide are loosened. The net effect contributes to the assault on the stability of the self.

The question 'Who are you?' may provoke any or all of the following answers:

◆   I am a worker—I have an occupation, a profession.

◆   I have a home town.

◆   I am a member of this family.

◆   I am a person with certain views about the world.

◆   I am a person who holds certain values.

But work, at least industrial or bureaucratic work, has tended to become dehumanized as it has been fragmented by the technology of industrial production—and threatens to disappear altogether as that process reaches the limits of its efficiency.

Occupations are far less durable than they were fifty or even twenty years ago. A man who defines himself as a chemical engineer, a shoemaker, or a specialist in internal medicine, runs an increasing risk of building identity on an unstable base. It is becoming less likely that occupational and professional identities will last throughout an entire lifetime. Traditional skills in such fields as machine tools and textiles have been rendered increasingly obsolete. A chemical engineer who grew up in the kind of chemical engineering proper to the paint or adhesive industry of thirty years ago, finds himself in sharply decreasing demand today. Specialists at the frontiers of research medicine are having to 'retool' at least every ten years in a way that is almost as intense as their original research training.

Regional stability is fast becoming a myth. A man who changes jobs on his way up may have to move his home, and the average young American family moves more than once. In addition, neighborhoods and regions that as little as thirty years ago provided a well-defined basis for regional identity, have been very nearly homogenized, in large part through the technology of the automobile, television, and consumer appliances, and through the systems that have been created to distribute and merchandise these products. Distinctions among persons tend to be socio-economic rather than based on region or neighborhood.

It becomes more difficult to cling to religious identity as religious institutions grope for new roles in society. The same is true of such quasi-religious institutions of the thirties as the labor movement.

The family fragments under the strain of competing institutions and invading technologies.

Identification with an organization suffers from the instability of the organizations themselves.

The corporation has been a salient institution for many of the men who work in it. But for most blue-collar workers, the corporation offers little basis for identity; it is rather an organization to be tolerated or outwitted in order to have access to consumer goods. For white-collar and professional workers, moving up means moving from job to job. Men may identify with their corporations, but they are likely to identify with several corporations in the course of a working lifetime. Even for someone who remains with his company for a long time, the nature of that company is apt to shift radically so that the effect is almost as though he were working for different companies.

Values undergo metamorphosis. As particular occupations, regions and organizations become threatened with disruption, values associated with them come into question. Broader cultural values—those associated with

the concepts of modernity, or social progress, for example
—lose their force partly as a consequence of the very
'success' (and resulting apparent emptiness) of the social
movements they represent. The Technological Program
showed us moving toward a posterity in which peace,
satisfaction, work, freedom, and stable identity were to be
attained through technological enterprise. But technological change has produced unintended and unanticipated effects which are monstrous. It has undermined
the very goals of the Technological Program, dehuman-
izing work, replacing individuality with mass society,
magnifying the threat to peace. What had appeared to
be an instrument capable of realizing human goals turns
out to set its own conditions and to impose its own values.

The most important feature of the threat to stable
institutions and to stable anchors for identity is the sense
in which they have caused us to lose faith in the stable
state itself.[4] Not only do we regard our established
institutions as inadequate to the challenges they face; we
find it increasingly difficult to believe in the feasibility of
developing new institutions which will be stable. Not
only have social values eroded; we do not believe in the
stability of the values we may be able to invent to replace
them. This phenomenon, the loss of the stable state,
carries with it its own reinforcement. If persons are to
respond to instability and uncertainty, they must, on
some basis, feel secure; a sense of personal security is
essential to our ability to come to grips with change. But
the very pervasiveness of the erosion of the stable state
undercuts the sources of support for personal security.
We have it least where we need it most.

The sources of threat to the stable state in our own time

The widespread sense that institutions throughout our
society are inadequate to meet the present challenge, and
that the anchors of personal identity are everywhere
being eroded, come from phenomena that seem to be in

some sense unique to our time. But it is not easy to say precisely what those phenomena are.

It is said that we are living in a time of disruptive transition. But there have been other times of transition and disruption: Greece during the Hellenistic period, Europe in the fifteenth century, the opening up of Japanese society in the late nineteenth century. The question remains whether there is anything unique about *this* period of disruption. What peculiar features of the last half-century or so have led, in modern industrial society and in particular in the United States, to the loss of the stable state?

It has become customary to observe that we are experiencing an unprecedented and accelerating rate of change, and to attribute this to accelerating technology. But there has been debate between those who argue that we are experiencing an increase in the rate of change which is in itself unique, and uniquely tied to technology, and those who assert that there is no difference between the rate of technological change we are now experiencing and the rate of technological change characteristic of the western world at any time during the last two hundred years.

The first argument rests on two forms of data. Curves can be drawn to show the growth of particular aspects of technological change (which may be called 'technological parameters') from the seventeenth or eighteenth centuries to the present time. These technological parameters may be chosen almost at random—velocity, propulsive force, the hardness and strength-to-weight ratio of materials, the number of chemical elements known, or the number of computations that can be performed in a second. Exponential* curves of growth characterize them all.

---

* An example of exponential growth is a town whose population trebles every ten years (3,000 in 1930, 9,000 in 1940, 27,000 in 1950 and so on). In general, an exponential curve is one formed by a series of points at fixed intervals each of which represents the same base raised to a higher power each time (e.g. $3, 3^2, 3^3 \ldots 3^n$).

Curves showing the length of time required for technological innovations to spread broadly throughout populations of users, suggest an exponential rate of shrinkage.

Invention	Time required for diffusion in years
steam engine	150–200
automobile	40–50
vacuum tube	25–30
transistor	about 15

The time required for the diffusion of major technological innovations would appear to be approaching zero
as a limit!

But a problem underlies these arguments.

Although the curves present the growth of science and
technology as exponential, this phenomenon is by no
means unique to our time.

> . . . the 80- to 90-per cent currency of modern science is a
> direct result of an exponential growth that has been steady
> and consistent for a long time. It follows that this result, true
> now, must also have been true *at all times in the past*, back to
> the eighteenth century and perhaps even as far back as the
> late seventeenth. In 1900, in 1800, and perhaps in 1700, one
> could look back and say that most of the scientists that have
> ever been are alive now, and most of what is known has been
> determined within living memory. In that respect, surprised
> though we may be to find it so, the scientific world is no
> different now from what it has always been since the seven-
> teenth century. Science has always been modern; it has
> always been exploding into the population, always on the
> brink of its expansive revolution . . . [5]

What is true of science is true of technology. Both have
grown exponentially and the law governing their rate of
change is the same as it has been for the last hundred or
two hundred years. Nevertheless, the actual number of
technological innovations impinging on our society each
year continues to grow. We are reaching ever greater

levels of scientific and technological activity and performance, both absolutely and in relation to the society as a whole. And the technological enterprise, as it reaches new levels, may also pass beyond certain social thresholds. If we are in a closed chamber whose carbon dioxide content is doubling every five hours, this pattern of change may hold as true at the third doubling as at the second—but on the third we may suffocate.

As it has gone its exponential way, technological change has become increasingly *pervasive*. Changes whose impacts might have been contained in particular industries, in particular regions or in particular aspects of life, now penetrate all industries, all regions and all of life.

The cluster of technological changes which make up industrialization have this effect. Coupled with the massive trends toward urbanization, spreading industrialization has meant that nearly all people in industrial nations live in an environment conditioned by the technology of industrial production and its offshoots. There are no rural or regional enclaves safe from industrialization. Similarly, the technology of the city, and most particularly the central technologies of automotive transportation, engulf industrial nations. Consequently, a large Spanish city has less the character of a Spanish city than of a modern, industrial city anywhere. Houses have become centers of domestic industrial production and more like one another in this respect than they are unlike in any other respect.

A second point, distinct from the first and equal to it in importance, is that these pervasive technologies have been unique in content. While every new technology is by definition unique, there are levels or degrees of novelty. Inventions fall into sequences of families, such as the families of inventions based on the steam engine or on movable type. The development of these technological veins proceeds through zones of continuity, and then, at intervals, there are discontinuities. In these technological revolutions[6] whole new veins of theory and phenomena emerge to be exploited by generations of new technology.

Much of the new technology since the turn of the century has been *implosive* in its effects. It has been 'infrastructure' technology, technology governing the flow of goods, people, money and information. The new electronic technologies of communications have, in particular, evolved as though they were going to produce, as a limiting state, the instantaneous confrontation of every part of our society with every other part. As a result, social inequities leap to universal attention. Every theory confronts its counter-instance. Conflicts long suppressed by separation and isolation escape the bounds that had confined them, and as new societies come into contact, new conflicts emerge.

The most powerful of the new technologies have been 'meta' technologies. Their effect has been to facilitate the processes of technological innovation and diffusion, and thereby to increase the society's leverage on technological change itself. Into this category fall the infrastructure technologies, along with the techniques of distribution and merchandising which depend on them; these have permitted the emergence of new systems for the diffusion of innovation. The invention of the organization of invention, first brought to visibility in the laboratory of Thomas Edison, has come into good currency with the spread of the large-scale industrial and government research laboratory. The technology of the computer carries with it potentials for the management of technological innovation and diffusion which have only begun to be tapped.

Technologies such as these have had an equally powerful but more subtle influence as *metaphors* for human activity. It is in this sense, for example, that Marshall McLuhan speaks of the development of 'a new tribalism' among the young stimulated not only by the implosiveness of television but by its influence as a metaphor for human interaction. In this sense, too, electronic technology stimulates new forms of organization based on the networks and grids of electronic devices, characterized by complex matrices of relationships rather than by simple lines of authority, and by the fact that information is available simultaneously at the crucial nodes of decision.

The shrinking interval between technological impacts on society means that adaptation cannot remain generational. Death has played an essential role in the evolution of human societies, just as it has in the evolution of all biological systems. Death is, after all, a necessary component in the process of natural selection; only as some individuals die off, while others survive to breed, do the traits of species evolve selectively over generations.

In human societies, generational change has often been the vehicle through which major cultural changes have occurred. Sons, replacing fathers, bring into use the new gifts of the culture which the fathers found too strange and threatening to use. In recent times, we need only think of the transitions from the family to the industrialized farm, or from the family business to the modern corporation.

As diffusion times have shrunk steadily from 120 to 60 to 30 to 15 years, problems of adaptation which could once have been handled—say, in the period between 1800 and 1920—through the conflict of generations and the replacement of one generation by another, must now be handled within a single generation. Individuals must somehow confront and negotiate, in their own persons, the transformations which used to be handled by generational change. We are no longer able to afford the relatively leisurely process of adaptation which has until now allowed us to keep the illusion of the stable state.

To sum up, we may say that, while technological change has been continuing exponentially for the last two hundred years, it has now reached a level of pervasiveness and frequency uniquely threatening to the stable state. And while all new technology is more or less disruptive, the implosiveness of the vein of technology mined in the last half-century has made it uniquely disruptive.

Responses to the loss of the stable state

The most prevalent responses to the loss of the stable state are anti-responses. They do not confront the challenge directly. They seek instead to deny it, to escape it or to become oblivious to it. The anti-responses take three primary forms:

Return 'Let us return to the last stable state.' This is the response of reaction against an intolerable present.

Recently I heard an old farmer in Oklahoma say that he had been farming for forty years and felt he had become something of an expert on the subject. It was his considered opinion that farmers had gone from milking 10 to 20 to 40 cows a day without increasing income, only running to stand still. All this was the fault of the Agricultural Extension Service, and of technological progress in general. Sooner or later we would have to return to the concept of the family farm.

Localism is a special case of return. It is an attempt to enforce and sustain isolation from the phenomena that threaten established institutions and values. Since the cherished past survives in an enclave, the drive to return takes the form of an attempt to protect the integrity of that enclave—as in the State of Mississippi at the present time.

Revolt There is a form of revolutionary response whose warcry is total rejection of the past and of all vestiges of the past in existing social systems. The characteristic movement of this form of revolt is against established institutions rather than toward a vivid and well-worked-out ideal. In this sense, direction comes from the established institutions themselves and the past sneaks in the back door.

This form of 'reactionary radicalism' moves *against*, sustains energy only as long as there is a target.[7] It flourishes on the energy generated by the process of revolution itself.

Mindlessness This is an attempt to escape from anguish and uncertainty by evading reflective consciousness itself. The methods may be drugs, hypnotic routine, violence, or a peculiar union with machine technology— like the kids in midwestern American towns who tool around empty squares at night on motorcycles or in hot rods and seem to be saying, 'The machine is winning. Why not join it?'

The anti-responses share a failure to confront what it might be like to live without the stable state. For them the loss of the stable state is like a gorgon's head, too dreadful to be contemplated. And they are destructive responses. Return is futile; there is nothing to go back to. Revolt, in the form of reactionary radicalism, represents a perverse return under the mask of violence. Mindlessness avoids the dreaded reality only by giving up awareness and humanity.[8]

Constructive responses to the loss of the stable state must confront the phenomenon directly. They must do so at the level of the institution and of the person.

- ◆ If our established institutions are threatened with disruption, how can we invent and bring into being new or modified institutions capable of confronting challenges to their stability without freezing and without flying apart at the seams?

- ◆ If we are losing stable values and anchors for personal identity, how can we maintain a sense of self-respect and self-identity while in the very process of change?

The present work is an effort to come to grips with these questions. It proceeds on the following assumptions:

- The loss of the stable state means that our society and all of its institutions are in *continuing* processes of transformation. We cannot expect new stable states that will endure even for our own lifetimes.

- We must learn to understand, guide, influence and manage these transformations. We must make the capacity for undertaking them integral to ourselves and to our institutions.

- We must, in other words, become adept at learning. We must become able not only to transform our institutions, in response to changing situations and requirements; we must invent and develop institutions which are 'learning systems', that is to say, systems capable of bringing about their own continuing transformation.

- The task which the loss of the stable state makes imperative, for the person, for our institutions, for our society as a whole, is to learn about learning.

    What is the nature of the process by which organizations, institutions and societies transform themselves?

    What are the characteristics of effective learning systems?

    What are the forms and limits of knowledge that can operate within processes of social learning?

    What demands are made on a person who engages in this kind of learning?

These are the questions we will be asking in the pages that follow.

2 Dynamic conservatism

In *Men, Machines and Modern Times*[1] the American historian Elting Morison tells the story of the introduction into the US Navy of continuous-aim firing—a method of keeping guns trained on an enemy ship when both your ship and the enemy's are moving up and down and steaming in different directions at the same time.

The Navy's standard method, in Theodore Roosevelt's time employed a very heavy set of gears and a highly trained crew with a kind of football coach/naval captain who gave directions to the crew. Although there was a gunsight, nobody dared put his eye to it because of the recoil of the gun. Sims, a young naval officer, developed a new method which took advantage of the inertial movement of the ship; he simplified the gearing procedure and isolated the sight from recoil, so that it became possible for the operator to keep his eye on the sight and move the gears at the same time. He tested his system and was able to effect a remarkable increase in accuracy.

Sims then wrote to Naval Headquarters, with the aim of having his device officially adopted throughout the fleet, and the Navy wrote back that it was not interested. But Sims had the persistence characteristic of technological innovators and he finally persuaded the Navy to test his method of continuous-aim firing. The test, as devised by the Navy, consisted in strapping the device to a solid block in the Navy Yard in Washington where, deprived of the inertial movement of the ship, it failed, proving scientifically that continuous-aim firing was not feasible. Sims was not deterred. Finally, he reached President Theodore Roosevelt directly, and the President forced the device down the Navy's throat. Under these conditions the Navy accepted it, and achieved a remarkable increase in accuracy in all theatres.

Morison points out that the Navy understandably tried to protect the social system of the ship from a technology which was in fact destructive of it. By introducing continuous-aim firing, Sims threatened a specialized, highly trained team, replacing it with an operation in which, in effect, any recruit could serve.

The example is characteristic of social systems, whether a naval ship, an industrial firm, or a community.

The system as a whole has the property of resistance to change. I would not call this property 'inertia,' a metaphor drawn from physics—the tendency of objects to move steadily along their present courses unless a contrary force is exerted on them. The resistance to change exhibited by social systems is much more nearly a form of 'dynamic conservatism'—that is to say, a tendency to fight to remain the same.

So pervasive and central is this characteristic that it distinguishes social systems from other social groupings. A social system is a complex of individuals which tends to maintain its boundaries and its patterns of internal relationships. But given internal tendencies towards increasing disorder,[2] and external threats to stability, energy must be expended if the patterns of the system are to be held stable. Social systems are self-reinforcing systems which strive to remain in something like equilibrium. As Walter Cannon remarks about living systems,

> In an open system, such as our bodies represent, compounded of unstable material and subjected continually to disturbing

conditions, constancy is itself evidence that agencies are acting, or ready to act, to maintain this constancy. . . . If a state
remains steady it does so because any tendency toward
change is automatically met by increased effectiveness of the
factors which resist change.[3]

It is always futile to seek a single 'cause' for a system's
being the way it is. There is always a complex of interacting components. The social system contains structure,
technology and theory. The structure is the set of roles
and relations among individual members. The theory
consists of the views held within the social system about
its purposes, its operations, its environment and its
future. Both reflect, and in turn influence, the prevailing
technology of the system. These dimensions all hang together so that any change in one produces change in the
others. In their interactions, they reinforce one another
and are aspects of the system's 'cause'.

Structure   In a business firm the organization chart
reflects social structure—the hierarchy of functional
departments (accounting, production, marketing and
the like) and their formal channels of interaction.
Structure consists in the relationships of control and
interaction among functional units.

The finer-grained structure of a social system reveals
individual roles and their relationships. Roles like
'worker,' 'manager,' 'analyst,' 'actor,' 'boss,' 'builder,'
are universals which apply to many different individuals;
quite different social systems contain the same or similar
roles. Within a business firm a role is defined, in a limited
and formal sense, by a description which includes
position within the system, criteria for the functions to be
carried out from that position, and relations to others
within the system. But roles also carry with them attri-
butes of status, commitments to theories and values—as
in the case of 'professional roles'—and they are loci for
perspectives on the broader system and on the outside
world.

Social structure and function are often ill-matched. The ponderous bureaucracy of an old organization tends to be badly suited to the problems created by any new situation. But social systems have informal structures which reflect how things actually work, rather than how they are supposed officially to work, and through informal structure organizations can often respond to situations for which their formal structures are unsuited. Agencies supposed to work together but incapable of doing so formally, may be able to do so through informal friendships or trading relationships.

A particular social structure will impose norms of behavior and the means of applying them—in a very broad sense, government. Families and neighborhoods, as well as organizations and agencies, have informal governments or networks which may be more or less congruent with formal government. 'The old man' may make the final decisions regardless of what the organization chart says.

If we think of a social system as an organism, formal and informal structures show the way in which the materials of the system are ordered. And, as with organisms, a social system's behavior reflects its structure.

Theory When a person enters a social system, he encounters a body of theory which more or less explicitly sets out not only the 'way the world is' but 'who we are,' 'what we are doing,' and 'what we should be doing.'

The theory of an industrial firm, for example, includes what the business is, how it works, what the market and the competition are like, and what kinds of performance are valued. The theory of an agency for the blind includes notions about what a blind person can learn to do, what is an appropriate service, what professional behavior consists in, the difference between good and bad clients, what the objectives of providing service are.

Social systems have both formal and informal theory.

The formal or official theory of an agency may revolve around the ideology of service and the professional code; the informal or hidden theory may include notions of processing clients through the system, keeping clients within the orbit of the agency, and producing data that satisfy the federal monitors.

While the broad theory of the social system may be shared by everyone in it, there are likely to be variants held by people in different parts of the structure. The cop on the beat and the police commissioner have different views of the world and of the police force. Workers on the assembly line, foremen and managers of production all have world views different from one another and from the world view of the president of the firm.

Value systems correspond to, and are inseparable from, theory. Within the theory of an industrial firm, there are values related to the maintenance of profit margins, share of market, quality of product, reduction in cost of operations, and satisfying the stockholders. And there may be informal values related to the culture of the company—for example, values placed on smooth relations between people, life tenure for employees, and minimal contact with outsiders.

It is in a way misleading to distinguish at all between social system and theory, for the social system is the embodiment of its theory and the theory is the conceptual dimension of the social system.

Technology   A social system employs tools and techniques which extend the human capability of its members.

The technologies of the business firm include both tools of production, like lathes, drill-presses, and grinders, and techniques like market research and cost control. The household has its technologies. They include the house itself, with its mechanical systems; the utensils used in eating, sleeping, and washing; the tools and techniques associated with maintenance of the house and its grounds; and the techniques employed by members of the household as they keep clean, shop, and bring up children. An agency for the blind has its own tools—braille books, for example, and the long cane—as well as the techniques of rehabilitation, training and management practiced by the agency staff.

A social system has both 'hard' technologies (the physical tools) and 'soft' (the techniques and programs practiced by its members). There are technologies shared broadly among social systems—spectacles, for example, and automobiles—and there are technologies special to the social system, such as the housewife's stove and cook-book or the machinist's micrometer.

Social structure, theory and technology are interdependent. They have evolved in relation to one another, and they are built on one another. Hence, one cannot be changed without inducing change in the others.

A change in technology carries with it changes in social structure and in theory. Elting Morison's story of the introduction of continuous-aim firing shows how a new technology caused shifts to occur both in the hierarchy and the theory of the naval ship. The widespread introduction of household appliances has provided housewives with mechanical slaves, responding to and hastening the elimination of the domestic servant, freeing women for as yet uninvented roles, thereby intensifying the issue of woman's role and her relation to husband and children in the society of the family. Similarly, the flat, tribal culture of the young has emerged along with the electronic technologies of rock music, the drug scene, and the communications devices on which the youth 'network' depends: it is impossible to say which of these produced the other.

The theories of the Welfare State underlying the program of Social Security were among the factors that caused us to draw on emerging computer technology in the fifties to establish a computerized system of payments and accounts. The gradual infiltration of the concepts of marketing and merchandising into American politics, coupled with the full-scale development of television, brought into being political market research, computer simulation of the voting process and computerized forecasting of the vote.

The story of the introduction and diffusion of the automobile is perhaps the best documented illustration of this multiple interdependence of theory, structure and technology. Automobiles led to the creation of suburbs, which in turn changed the prevailing theories of the function of cities (no longer as places to live *and* work) and set in motion a broad-ranging pattern of decentralization of virtually all services and supplies. The belts and rings around our large cities gave rise to new concepts of industrial location and development which tended in turn to isolate those still living in center cities. The very concept of 'center city' grew up in response to developments brought about by the automobile. Many small, isolated 'estates' grew up in the suburbs, transforming the structure of neighborhoods as they had existed in the cities. The relative isolation of the suburban house called into being a complex of services and led to a suburban culture which has been, in many ways, the breeding ground for the present youth culture.

It is apparent, in all of this, how misleading it is to speak of the 'social consequences of technological change'—as though 'society' and 'technology' were separate to begin with. Every social system mirrors a technological plenum. There is never an absence of technology, but always the particular technology around which the social system has developed. New technology does not enter a vacuum but displaces prevailing technology and, in so doing, leads to chain reactions in structure, theory and values.

Social systems resist change with an energy roughly proportional to the radicalness of the change that is threatened. It is useful, following the lead of the psychologist Abraham Maslow, to picture a social system as a kind of ring structure.

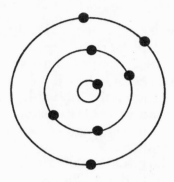

At the periphery are those elements whose change would require least disruption of the system as a whole. At the center are those elements whose change would mean restructuring the entire system.

Within the society of the household, small changes in hairstyle, eating habits, patterns of sleep and waking, leave the system relatively intact. But a shift in role which makes the woman breadwinner rather than housewife shakes the system to its roots. Within the society of the military, the introduction of the helicopter as a weapon has altered operations, roles, training and strategies of operation, but it has left the structure of military society pretty much unchanged. A shift away from the system of rank and authority as a principle of organization, however, would change it to the point of making it unrecognizable.

What is true of the theories embodied in social systems is also true of theories generally. W. V. O. Quine has called attention to a similar phenomenon in the realm of mathematics and logic:

... the more fundamental a law is to our conceptual scheme, the less likely we are to choose it for revision. When some revision of our system of statements is called for, we prefer, other things being equal, a revision which disturbs the system least. ... The priority on law, considered now apart from any competition with the priority on statements verified by experience, admits of many gradations. Conjectures of history and economics will be revised more willingly than laws of physics, and these more willingly than laws of mathematics and logic. ... Mathematics and logic, central as they are to the conceptual scheme, tend to be accorded such immunity, in view of our conservative preference for revisions which disturb the system least; and herein, perhaps, lies the 'necessity' which the laws of mathematics and logic are felt to enjoy.[4]

Everything we have so far remarked about resistance to change may be turned around to help in planning strategies of intervention. Given the interdependence of structure, theory and technology, any one of them may be chosen as a route to change in a social system. And the more radical the change to be introduced, the more central must be the element of structure, theory or technology we attack. We discover the complexity and depth of a system's dynamic conservatism by seeking to change it.

The American Building Industry

The patterns of dynamic conservatism reveal themselves best in the course of particular efforts at change.

In 1963, Herbert Hollomon and several colleagues in the US Department of Commerce attempted to launch the Civilian Industrial Technology Program, a program concerned with the plight of 'backward' industries whose support for research and development lagged far behind their contribution to Gross National Product. These were technologically deficient industries, most of them dating from the Industrial Revolution. They were made up of a few large firms and many thousands of small ones; they had low margins of profit and they made little investment in technology.

The building industry was considered to be a backward industry of this kind, although its fragmentation and dispersion led to some doubt about its being an industry at all. A report had been prepared which documented the general absence of building research in the United States. Although building material suppliers did some research on components and materials, there was little or no research, for example, on the problem of housing for low-income families. A conclusion of the report, and a part of the CIT program, was that government should undertake and stimulate building research.

The industry responded to this proposal. Prominent industry spokesmen called it a socialist program aimed at destroying the free enterprise system. They said that the way to right the balance of Federal support for research and development was not to shore up the backward industries, but to reduce support to the space and defense industries, which were receiving too much support. Further, more research was going on than had been uncovered; an independent industry-sponsored study showed a total research budget of $1 million in 1962, most of it devoted to product development.

A representative of one of the principal industrial associations made clear his wish to control the CIT program. Failing that, he would kill the program and get its proponents fired. His performance appeared to be an amusing piece of bravado. But he was able to do almost exactly what he threatened. And in doing so, he revealed a great deal about the complex and dynamically conservative building industry system.

The building industry includes:

- Building contractors and suppliers of building materials and their associations, ranging from the

Iron and Steel Institute to the National Association of Home Builders

◆ Architects, engineers and their associations

◆ Craft labor unions, on national and local levels

◆ Speculative developers

◆ Building code inspectors

◆ Federal and local government purchasers of buildings, building equipment and supplies (such as the Bureau of Public Roads and the Army Corps of Engineers) and their associations

◆ Bankers and financiers

◆ An active and diversified building press

◆ A few bodies such as the Building Research Institute and the Building Research Advisory Board, which attempt to make and influence policy for the industry as a whole.

What Hollomon's little effort at encouraging building research had done was to lift the center of this web, so that it began to be possible to see the connections between apparently separate elements of the system. It turned out that building suppliers, craft unions, code inspectors, purchasers, contractors, and virtually the whole array of building industry units, make up a coalition of shared interests built on prevailing technologies. Unions, for example, have developed a system of operations based on bricks as a construction material, which overlaps in most particulars the interests of the brick manufacturers themselves. A call to research sounds like a call to replacement of bricks as a building material and therefore like a threat to these multiple interests. For not only suppliers and unions, but contractors, building inspectors, purchasers, the building press (through advertisers) and government agencies that set standards for the approval of mortgages

—all have an investment in the technology of bricks. Their livelihoods, the ways of working with which they are familiar, and the standards they know how to write and enforce, depend on the prevailing technology,which is based on the brick.

These representatives of the building industry connect to the official channels of government. The building materials spokesmen contacted a congressman from Ohio (Ohio is a major base for the structural clay tile industry) who sat on the Appropriations Sub-committee. This committee, chaired by Congressman John Rooney of Brooklyn, handles appropriations for the Department of Commerce. Rooney was always on the alert for weapons with which to punish the Department—he had made and lived on a reputation as 'Mr Economy'—and he gladly seized on the industry's opposition to the CIT program.

Through connections between the industry and Congress, the industry spokesman succeeded in limiting the CIT program to a small, short-term appropriation for textiles. And he very nearly succeeded in firing the initiators of the program.

There is a dynamism which is sometimes on the level of unconscious activity and sometimes on the level of a conscious conspiracy to employ the web of building industry connections to maintain the industry's stable state.[5] Its aim is to prevent the introduction of new technology and new institutions if these appear to threaten the industry's social and economic arrangements.

What is true of the Navy and the building industry tends to be true of all established institutions. It is true, for example, of the system of services to the blind.

The blindness system

This is a complex that includes:

◆ the set of persons with severe visual impairments

- the set of agencies, groups, and institutions that serve and support them
- the research and training that affect the provision of services
- the laws, policies and programs under which services are provided.

To call all of this a 'system' is not to imply that it has well-defined, consensual goals and coordinated programs for reaching them. The institutions included in the blindness system tend, in fact, to behave in a fragmented and disorganized way. In this sense, it is a *non-system*. Nevertheless, all the components listed above are relevant to the experience of the blind in the United States.

Agencies specifically concerned with the blind exist in the US at Federal, State and local levels. They fall into two parallel systems, one public and the other private—although the clarity of this distinction has been eroded in recent years as private agencies have sought and received more public funds. There are approximately 800 agencies for the blind. They differ with respect to the services they provide and the basis on which they are organized. Some specialize in particular functions, such as aid to the needy blind or residential schools for the blind. Others are large agencies with many functions. Still others are consulting agencies or producers and distributors of materials for the blind.

In addition to the providers of services, there are special 'sub-systems' concerned with research, both medical and non-medical, and with manpower training.

All of this is the *official* blindness system which provides services specifically to the blind under the heading of blindness. There is, beyond that, a substantial *unofficial* system which provides benefits or services to the blind under headings other than blindness: for example, the systems involved with welfare, social security, veterans' benefits, and health.

Finally, there is an *informal* blindness system which consists of services to the blind provided by no established agencies, but by families, friends and neighbors.

The history of blindness in the United States shows a significant evolution in the groups of people identified as blind.

In the period between 1900 and the 1930s the blind consisted primarily of children, and adults of working age. The dominant causes of blindness were war, industrial accident, and diseases affecting children and adults of varying age groups. The blind were likely to have blindness as their only handicap.

In the 1930s, as part of the wave of action on social welfare that swept over the country, federal and state aid to the blind came into being on a significant scale. The *sheltered workshop*, publicly or privately supported, trained blind adults for occupations thought to be particularly appropriate—piano tuner, broom-maker, or vending stand operator, for example. *The school for the blind* provided separate-track, segregated education for the blind child.[6] In the early 1940s, legislation on *vocational rehabilitation* began to bring into being a broad array of state-based agencies for the blind. These focused primarily on rehabilitating adults of working age. Their central test of rehabilitation was that a client should be fit to work and so achieve economic independence.

From 1900 to the present time, the make-up of the blind population has changed. That of the severely visually impaired in the United States is now heavily weighted toward

- the aged blind
- the multiple-handicapped, especially among blind children
- the poor, ethnic minorities, the low-skilled
- those with significant residual vision.

All sources of data, however much they conflict in other ways, show a high percentage of people over 65. A higher percentage of blind *women* goes together with increase in the numbers of those over 65, as does an increase in the percentage of blind people with significant residual vision, for blindness in the aged tends to come on gradually. Similarly, the dominant causes of blindness become senile degeneration, diabetes and multiple etiologies character- istic of old age; and prenatal influence which tends to be associated with other disabilities in addition to blindness. The overall pattern, both for the aged and for children, is one of multiple disability. And projections to 1970 and 1985 suggest that, with increasing numbers of people over 65, these trends will continue.

The pattern makes economic employment an unrealis- tic goal for an increasing majority of the blind. Neverthe- less, almost all agencies for the blind continue to behave as though this shift in the blind population had not taken place. They measure their success in selecting clients and providing services by how far the clients achieve some degree of economic independence.

Not surprisingly, the official blindness system provides services to a relatively small fraction of those who are eligible for them. If services are limited to education, re- habilitation and care, those who receive them are esti- mated[7] to be about 20 per cent of the total blind popula- tion.

The 20 per cent served tend to be children with the single handicap of blindness, or adults of working age and potential for employment; they receive educational, reading, mobility and vocational services. The 80 per cent not served tend to be those without apparent poten- tial for employment or for educational advancement, the aged, the multiple-handicapped, the poor and low- skilled.[8] These persons tend either to be shunted off to other systems, to receive minimal income-maintenance or custodial care, or to be ignored.

The mix of services offered is relatively unresponsive to the changing characteristics, needs, interests and capacities of the blind. Services tend to be designed, for example, for those entirely without vision, in spite of the residual vision possessed by a growing majority of the blind. Agencies tend to behave as though the blind needed or should have the services offered by agencies, rather than that agencies should modify services in response to the changing needs or characteristics of the blind. The system has been, for the most part, unresponsive to the population of the blind, which has shifted out from under it.

Given what the blindness system would have to become if it were to encounter every blind person, and given the gross mismatch of the current system with the changing population of the blind, it is remarkable that the network of agencies has been able to keep its traditional modes of operation intact. But individual agencies have made the system as a whole dynamically conservative through their use of the variety of instruments available to them:

◆ *Control of the valve*
    Agencies can limit their services to 'good clients' and can actually seek out clients meeting their criteria. In large cities, for example, there is active competition for children who are blind only. And parents of such children often learn, as a result, to go 'agency shopping'.

◆ *Control of the duration of the client's stay*
    Agencies tend to keep 'good clients' for a longer period of time—for months instead of weeks, and not infrequently for years.

◆ *Control of the portion of the client's life space taken up by the agency*
    Agencies may extend their services not only to dis-

abilities directly relevant to blindness, such as those associated with reading or travel, but to the client's overall health, his family relations, his psychological well-being, and the like. At one extreme, the agency becomes the client's total environment.

◆ *Control of investment per client*
As scope of service and duration of stay increase, the agency increases its investments of dollars and manpower in individual clients.

Through the manipulation of these valves, agencies behave like homeostatic systems. They compensate for a declining population of the right sorts of clients by increasing the investment in the clients they do serve, all under the heading of improving the quality of service. As a consequence, the agency staff remains stable even though client populations decrease. The agency maintains its standards for clients even though the number of good clients decreases absolutely and in relation to the total number of blind. It behaves as though it were optimizing the use of its existing resources.

The homeostatic system is self-reinforcing and is, in a critical sense, its own cause. But it depends upon a number of factors which are both incentives to and means by which agencies maintain something like a stable state.

There is, for example, an ideology still in good currency among professionals within the blindness system. It centers on concern with *individuals* rather than with numbers, on high standards of service as defined within the field, on 'worthy' clients (where the blindness system is seen as deciding both what clients are worthy and what services they should receive) and on a concept of professionalism which defines appropriate behavior for user as well as for provider. All of this has great influence on the society of the blindness agencies. It both encourages and supports the homeostatic behavior of the agencies. After all, worthy clients deserve the highest quality of professional service; one need not be overly concerned with the numerous, invisible others.

The chaotic nature of information about the system functions as a defense against change. Further, most agencies systematically avoid follow-up—that is, avoid discovering what happens to their clients after service has been provided. As a consequence, the system is cut off and protected from the opportunity of learning.

All these factors serve to reinforce the homeostatic behavior of the agencies. Resistance to change does not come from the stupidity or venality of individuals within the system; it is a function of the system itself.

Strategies of dynamic conservatism

The examples of the Navy, the building industry and the blindness system barely scratch the surface of the variety and complexity of processes through which social systems practice dynamic conservatism.

For any given system and for any given threat there are, as I have suggested earlier, *sequences* of strategies which tend to follow a logic of their own—a logic as complex as the logic of homeostasis in biological organisms or the logic of 'resistance' and 'defense mechanism' as described by the Freudian psychoanalysts.

An oversimplified first response to the presence of a threat is to ignore it, a response for which Sullivan used the phrase 'selective inattention'. Anyone is familiar with the device who has tried to become part of a closed small group and has been unable to bring himself to the group's attention. Ralph Ellison illustrated the strategy in *The Invisible Man*: the negro was an invisible man because no one noticed him. But the response is very nearly universal. A stranger to an organization can usually notice things the organization has kept hidden from itself; this fact makes consulting possible.

When it is no longer possible to avoid noticing a threat, it may be possible to launch a counter-attack or

even a preventive attack before the threat has material-
ized. The nature of the counter-attack will depend not
only on the nature of the threat but also on the traditions
of the system; traditional responses to threat are, after all,
a part of the culture of any social system. The building
industry's response to the Civilian Industrial Technology
program is a case in point.

When the threat cannot be totally repulsed, or when it
is internal and cannot be eradicated, dynamic conservatism runs to strategies of containment and isolation. Allow
the threatened change a limited scope of activity and
keep it bottled up. If this strategy is practiced for some
time, it gives rise to compartmentalization. The system as
a whole breaks down into units or territories, each of
which walls itself off from the others. Compartmentalization arises also as a consequence of the territorial (and
counter-territorial) impulses of subsidiary systems, as in
the departmental structure of universities or the strata-
like bureaucracies of government agencies full of vestigial
pockets of activity left over from earlier administrations.

The organization pays a price for its successful strategies, whose results may prevent the system from making
adaptations essential to growth or to vitality. In fact, we
may see social structure as the palpable consequence of
strategies of dynamic conservatism. As D'Arcy Thompson
says, 'the form of an object is a "diagram of forces", in
this sense, at least, that from it we can judge of or deduce
the forces that are acting or have acted upon it.'[9]

Co-option, a recently fashionable term, refers to the process by which established social systems absorb agents of
change and de-fuse, dilute, and turn to their own ends
the energies originally directed towards change. But the
concept has a far longer history, going back to the strata-
gem of the conquered tribe which absorbed and appro-
priated the culture of the conquerors.

When processes embodying threat cannot be repelled,
ignored, contained or transformed, social systems tend to

respond by change—but by the *least change* capable of neutralizing or meeting the intrusive process. 'Least' and 'greatest' are to be understood here in terms suggested earlier—namely, in terms of how little or how much must be given up in order to accommodate them. Nominalistic or token changes are of this order: an old department may be renamed in the terms of the rhetoric of change.[10]

In all these cases, the response is similar—minimal compliance with the demand for change. It is particularly effective where those pressing for change cannot distinguish significant from token compliance, or can muster their forces only for an initial assault. In this respect, established social systems have the advantage; they are able to exert continuing energy in the service of their stable state, whereas those attacking can seldom sustain their attack.

As social systems do begin to change in response to some form of effective threat, their response need not continue in the mode of least change. In practice they do not usually yield ground in a steady series of small steps. The dynamics of yielding are similar to the dynamics of change, of which they are the obverse. A system's early adaptations to change may follow the tactic of least change: if the threats persist and are effective, changes of state may be sudden and massive.

The roots of dynamic conservatism

It would be tempting to identify dynamic conservatism simply with the villanous machinations of vested interests. But this would be a drastic over-simplification.

In his study of the introduction of continuous-aim firing, Elting Morison relates these forces of dynamic conservatism to the understandable self-interest of individuals throughout the hierarchy of a naval ship. 'Military organizations are societies built around and upon the prevailing weapons systems. Intuitively and quite correctly the military man feels that a change in weapons portends a change in the arrangement of this society.'[11] The dynamic conservatism of the system as a whole results from the workings of self-interest in those individuals who are able to see the connection between their own self-interest and the interests of the social system as a whole.

This explanation is powerful. It helps to trace the multiple connections between technological change or the threat of it and the social structure of institutions in which innumerable self-interests have their base. But it does not do justice to the tenacity and rigidity of resistance to social change. It does not adequately account for what appears to be the non-rational character of that resistance. After all, a reorganized naval ship has not failed to remain a naval ship. Since the introduction of continuous-aim firing, a modified social structure of the ship has managed to keep itself in being through several wars and several even more threatening periods of peace.

What is more, dynamic conservatism is by no means always attributable to the stupidity of individuals within social systems, although their stupidity is frequently invoked by those seeking to introduce change. But why, then, should systems fail to reflect the intelligence of their members? The power of social systems over individuals becomes understandable, I think, only if we see that social systems provide for their members not only sources of livelihood, protection against outside threat and the promise of economic security, but a framework of theory, values and related technology which enables individuals to make sense of their lives. Threats to the social system threaten this framework.

A social system does not move smoothly from one state of its culture to another. In processes of social transformation, societies move from a relatively stable state through a zone of disruption to a new zone of relative stability. Something old must come apart in order for something new to come together. But for individuals within the system, there is no clear grasp of the *next* stable state—

only a clear picture of the one to be lost. Hence, the coming apart carries uncertainty and anguish for the members of the system, since it puts at risk the basis for self-identity that the system had provided.

It does not matter, then, if change may be seen in retrospect to have been harmless or even beneficial. Before the fact, the threat of disruption plunges individuals into an uncertainty more intolerable than any damage to vested interest. The self then puts its own conservative energies at the service of the system's conservation.

Some consequences for change and intervention

Social change in the broadest sense means simply change in any element of a social system over time. But there is also 'change of state' or 'transformation'—change in the total structural and cultural configuration of the system. To use earlier language, this is the sort of change that comes from the most radical modifications in elements of structure, theory or technology.

Malinowski speaks in this way about culture change:

> *Culture change* is the process by which the existing order of a society, that is, its social, spiritual and material civilization, is transformed from one type into another. Culture change thus covers the more or less rapid processes of modification in the political institutions of a society; in its domestic institutions and its modes of territorial settlement; in its beliefs and systems of knowledge; in its education and law; as well as in its materials tools and their use, and the consumption of goods on which its social economy is based. In the widest sense of the term, culture change is a permanent factor of human civilization; it goes on everywhere and at all times.[12]

His unit of change is the 'society', and 'transformation from one type into another' requires change in what he takes to be the critical dimensions of social organization.

Rostow, in *The Stages of Economic Growth*, envisages societies as economic systems and formulates economic development as a passage from one state of the system to another.

> Here then, in an impressionistic rather than an analytic way, are the stages of growth which can be distinguished once a traditional society begins its modernization: the transitional period when the preconditions for take-off are created generally in response to the intrusion of a foreign power, converging with certain domestic forces making for modernization; the take-off itself; the sweep into maturity generally taking up the life of about two further generations; and then, finally, if the rise of income has matched the spread of technological virtuosity . . . the diversion of the fully mature economy to the provision of durable consumers' goods and services (as well as the welfare state) for its increasingly urban—and then suburban—population. . . .[13]

In his manual on guerilla warfare, Che Guevara describes the transformation of the guerilla band as it perseveres in the war of liberation.

> At the outset there is a more or less homogeneous group, with some arms, that devotes itself almost exclusively to hiding in the wildest and most inaccessible places, making little contact with the peasants. It strikes a fortunate blow and its fame grows. A few peasants, dispossessed of their land or engaged in a struggle to conserve it, and young idealists of other classes join the nucleus; it acquires greater audacity and starts to operate in inhabited places, making more contact with the people in the zone; it repeats attacks, always fleeing after making them. . . . Men continue to join it; it has increased in number, but its organization remains exactly the same.
>
> Later it sets up temporary camps for several days. . . . The numbers in the guerilla band increase as work among the masses operates to make of each peasant an enthusiast for the war of liberation. Finally, an inaccessible place is chosen, a settled life is initiated, and the first small industries begin to be established; a shoe factory, a cigar and cigarette factory. . .
>
> The guerilla band now has an organization, a new structure. It is the head of a large movement with all the characteristics

of a small government. A court is established for the administration of justice, possibly laws are promulgated. . . . A moment arrives when its radius of action will not have increased
in the same proportion as its personnel; at that moment a
force of appropriate size is separated . . . and this goes to another place of combat.[14]

When change of state takes place in a tribal society, an
economic system or a guerilla movement, there are corresponding differences in the critical characteristics of
the system. But in every case there is transformation from
one type of configuration to another. And in every case
one must distinguish peripheral or even substantial
changes from the transformation of the system as a whole.

Changes in state have characteristic dynamic patterns.
Social systems move from zones of stability, through
zones of instability, to new stable zones. The zones of
instability can be considered transients. Movement of the
system from one stable state to another requires an input
of energy. But the system's response to this input varies
over time.

- There are *thresholds* of change—critical levels of
  energy which must be reached in order to precipitate change of state. Action on the system may have
  no perceptible effect until it reaches this threshold
  level.

- There are zones of *saturation* in which the rate of
  change begins to level off.

- Between these two sections of the curve, there is a
  zone of *exponential rise* in which the process 'goes
  critical', or becomes self-sustaining.

Dynamic conservatism helps to account for these phenomena. For any given system, it takes a certain level of
energy to overcome the forces involved in the system's
dynamic conservatism and to 'break' the stable state.
Once the threshold has been reached, the system goes in-

to exponential change until it reaches a new zone at which a new dynamic conservatism begins to operate; at this point, the continued application of energy has a diminishing effect.

Because of its dynamic conservatism, a social system is unlikely to undertake its own change of state. Because it sees every effort at transformation as an attack, transformation becomes a kind of war. Major shifts in the system come about in response to the system's failure or to the threat of failure—as political revolution may succeed a period of economic disaster, or as total corporate reorganization may succeed near ruin.

The energy required to reach the threshold of transformation takes the form of disruption and leads to crisis. Crisis consists in the system's actual or threatened inability to perform its essential functions for people in the system. Disruption is its cause and consequence.

Crises for the established institutions of our time come about naturally as the situations around which they were designed shift out from under them. But they are also subject to outside intervention, and when this succeeds in changing their state it takes the forms of insurgency and invasion, making the history of significant innovation a history of guerilla movements from within and invasions from without.

Insurgency throws into prominence the roles of champion, guerilla, entrepreneur, and revolutionary.

◆   The history of major technological innovation in the United States armed forces—from Theodore Roosevelt's time to the present day—reveals a series of individuals who challenged the system, were irrationally committed to the inventions they championed, operated informally and subversively, exploited informal internal networks and mobilized outside pressures, engaged in life-long combat, and became heroes or martyrs to their cause. The examples range from Goddard's rocketry to McLean's Sidewinder missile, Commander Hoover's 'ribbon in the sky', Rickover's atomic submarine and Gavin's Sky Cavalry.

♦ Carlson's battle to establish xerography, Land's entrepreneuring of polaroid photography, Sarnoff's championing of color television, all display variants of the embattled 'loner' who becomes an adversary of the system (of a firm or of an entire industry) in order to innovate.

Instances could as well be drawn from medicine, education, the labor movement, the church, or indeed from any established institution. At the root of most innovations significant enough to precipitate a change of state, there are individuals who display irrational commitment, extraordinary energy, a combativeness which enables them to battle established interests over long periods of time, and a remarkable skill at guerilla warfare.

Invasion includes a very large family of processes through which sources outside a system move across boundaries, bringing change in their wake.

♦ In literal, warlike invasion, one nation, tribe or society moves in on another, seeking to overcome it. Change may be self-induced, to ward off or counter invasion, or it may come about as invading and invaded societies interact, one imposing an order on the other or seeding the other with the elements of its culture.

♦ In a metaphorical sense, outsiders may invade an old organization, one industry may invade another. Over the last fifty years, major technological innovations in the traditional industries born in the first Industrial Revolution have followed invasions by newer, science-based industries. Chemical,

petrochemical, electronic and information-processing industries have moved into markets held by
paper, textile and machine-tool industries, carrying
with them synthetic fibers and finishes, plastics, and
numerically controlled machine tools.

◆ Migrants carry innovations across the boundaries
of social systems. Consider, for example, the impact
of successive waves of European, Oriental and
African migrants on the development of American
society; of the war-inspired emigration of German
scientists and scholars on American science and
culture; or of Southern negro migrants on the
culture of American cities.

◆ Cultural travellers move among societies, institutions and disciplines, carrying elements of one culture to another, as travelling artists, scholars, war-
riors and troubadours did in medieval Europe; as
workers carry the technology of one industry to
another; as political activists carry political experience from nation to nation; and as scholars and
scientists in their interdisciplinary travels cause
elements of their old disciplines to transform the
new. During World War II, British and American
professors of natural science and mathematics un-
dertook new kinds of weapons analysis around
problems such as bomb tracking and submarine
search, which led to the creation of the new disci-
pline called Operations Research. Their subsequent movement back into the ranks of business
and industry led to the diffusion of Operations
Research throughout society as a whole.

Invasions, whatever their form, bring about the transformation of social systems by carrying elements of a
foreign culture across the boundaries of the system, causing those elements to transform and to be transformed.

Invasion and insurgency, and the roles associated with them, belong to a broader family of roles and strategies of intervention, all based on recognition of the dynamic conservatism of social systems and on the need to transform through disruption and crisis. They share a vision of change as a kind of war and employ the language of power. They have their origins in a variety of organizational experiences, embody widely disparate paradigms of change, but share common roots in religion. The family includes

- The manager who 'turns his organization around' or 'drives it from above'

- The champion, who works within the organization, usually at lower levels, to press for new courses of action

- The guerilla, the champion gone underground, who tries to subvert the existing institution through informal channels

- The advocate, who represents and seeks a voice for the powerless

- The organizer, who unites individuals around issues of common concern in order to bring pressures to bear on established institutions

- The revolutionary who seeks, in open or hidden warfare, to overturn existing patterns of authority

- The consultant, teacher, or bard, who transmits the seeds of one culture to another.

All of these roles put the individual at risk. He must engage an essentially alien culture, and leave himself vulnerable to punishment for disrupting established power. All of these roles, therefore, make enormous demands on the person. They subject him to stresses he is able to meet only through a missionary stance.

There is, at least in American society, a very great attraction to the idea of the missionary. The role draws on deep commitment to a message, a sense of vocation to transmit that message, and a willingness—indeed, an eagerness—to encounter the daggers of an alien culture. The message of those who intervene in the roles of insurgency and invasion may be political, technological or organizational, but the quality of the commitment to the message and the concept of a life built around it are in the missionary mode.

Recognition of dynamic conservatism explodes the rational myth of intervention pervasive in official rhetoric, which envisages social change as a process made up of analysis of objectives, examination of alternatives, and selection of the most promising routes to change. Quite apart from its questionable claims to knowledge, the rational myth assumes implicitly that transformation occurs in a vacuum rather than in the plenum of self-reinforcing systems. Variants of the myth assume that rational plans will implement themselves, or they leave the question of implementation to a mysterious process of sales, persuasion, or politics.

Actual patterns of transformation center around crisis and reveal variations of invasion and insurgency. Concepts of roles and strategies of intervention suited to dynamic conservatism recognize the warlike and disruptive character of change.

Consequences for learning systems

The contents of the last two chapters, taken together, yield a disturbing message.

Through dynamic conservatism, institutions may survive in the face of their mismatch to the situations in which they function. But in a period when the stable state has been lost, the forms taken by dynamically conservative institutions condemn them to increasing irrelevance.

Or, if the loss of the stable state means that dynamically conservative institutions must yield to change of state, and if they can do so only through crisis and disruption, then we must look forward to a period of continuing disruption—to an era of perpetual coming apart.

These considerations set some conditions for learning systems. Social systems must learn to become capable of transforming themselves without intolerable disruption. But they will not cease to be dynamically conservative—not if dynamic conservatism is the process through which social systems keep from flying apart at the seams. A learning system, then, must be one in which dynamic conservatism operates at such a level and in such a way as to permit change of state without intolerable threat to the essential functions the system fulfils for the self. Our systems need to maintain their identity, and their ability to support the self-identity of those who belong to them, but they must at the same time be capable of frequently transforming themselves.

The movement toward learning systems is, of necessity, a groping and inductive process for which there is no adequate theoretical basis. In the chapters that follow, we will try to learn what we can from the clues provided by those emerging institutions which seem to have most light to throw on the nature of institutional learning.

◆ 3 Evolution of the business
◆ firm
◆

Business firms as learning systems

As we search for examples of learning systems, it is hard
to find a more striking example than the business firm.

To begin with, business firms in western society have
been primary vehicles for the diffusion of innovations and
therefore, in a major sense, agents of social learning for
society at large. Moreover, seen as a form evolving in
relation to its changing environment, the business firm
has been unsurpassed over the last fifty years in its ability
to effect rapid, inventive transformations of itself without flying apart at the seams, without disappearing as a
form, often without loss of identity even at the level of
the individual firm.

This pattern of evolution has proceeded in stages—
each marked by a characteristic 'defining concept' for
the firm, and by characteristic patterns of organization,
planning and management. The most recently emerging
stages represent, in effect, paradigms of learning systems
for the society as a whole.

The Standard Industrial Classification Manual reflects
the definition and organization of industries as they existed in the early years of this century. Industries were
defined around concepts like materials, energy, manufacture and transportation. The 'materials industry'
broke down, in turn, into the industries associated with
the production of specific materials—clay, paper, metals,

and the like. 'Manufacturing industries' clustered around specific classes of manufactured products like shoes, textiles, shops and toys. Within a manufacturing industry, a business firm defined itself by its 'product line', a subset of its industrial product category. Early on, these definitions corresponded to the actual structure of the industry.

The classical business firm

The classical business firm—the firm as it was understood in the first decades of this century—was organized around a product. Shoes are a case in point. A shoe as a product defines itself at the intersection of a particular kind of use or market and a particular technology. A company 'in the shoe business' had to have within it men who understood the technology of leather—who could tell, for example, by the feel, smell and look of a hide what its uses would be in manufacture; and such men came, not surprisingly, to dominate the industry. Within the firm, divisions formed around functions like production, sales, and accounting. The firm was an organizational pyramid with functional units under the control of functional managers and functional managers under the control of top management. The firm existed as an intermediate link in a chain of supply which fed into it raw and intermediate materials and manufacturing equipment, and a chain of distribution and marketing which carried its products to the ultimate consumer.

The classical business firm took as given its particular technology and the demand for its particular product. Planning, therefore, consisted primarily in the effort to match projected curves of supply and demand. The principal planning question has 'Will our capacity to produce match the readiness of the market to buy?'

From this early stage, the evolution of the business firm has had several major turning points.

The first of these occurred around World War II, a time in which certain broad transitional themes were announced: the shifts from static product-line to product innovation, from single product-line to product diversity, and from product-based to process-based definition of the firm. These transitions were brought about by a number of factors working together. They occurred in various industries at different rates and in different ways. And they brought about revolutionary changes in what it meant to be a business or an industry.

After World War II it began to become commonplace to think of invention as a necessary internal function of the firm. Previously, entrepreneurs had established businesses around inventions. Now it began to be an idea in good currency that regular and continuing invention was essential to the established firm. In part, this reflected the increasingly technological nature of industrial competition. In part, it responded to the twin ideologies of research and growth which had received much of their impetus from the example of the development and use of technology in the war. Finally, it reflected the increasing saturation of traditional markets and the need to create new markets by developing and marketing new products.

Business firms began to take seriously not only the improvement of technological and marketing systems associated with their existing product lines, but the internal generation of new businesses based on new product lines. The internalization of this development capability, initially seen as an instrument of corporate growth, turned out to require transformation of the nature of the firm itself; the tool transformed its user.

♦ *Firms raised the level of generality at which they defined their products.* 'Shoe companies' began to say that their business was 'footwear'; oil companies, 'energy'; business equipment firms, 'information processing'.

Where the change was not merely nominal, it signaled a broadening of the industrial base away

from the manufacture and sale of traditional products. A footwear company has within its scope the
manufacture and marketing of slippers, sneakers,
rubbers and boots, each built on a *different* technology. These are separate businesses, depending
on different materials, sources of supply, methods
of production, outlets, and channels of distribution.
No one could manage such a cluster of businesses
and integrate them into an effective whole, unless he
were able to give up the old 'shoe' mentality built
on the social and intellectual systems linked to the
technology of leather shoes. Such a business has a
charter for innovation far broader than newer and
better varieties of shoes. The marketing man is king
and the planners ask, 'Within the broad domain of
our market, what will they need? What will they
come to buy?'

◆   *Science-based industries, advanced in their ability to*
undertake and use research, invaded traditional industries.
The invasion of traditional industries dating from
the Industrial Revolution (textiles, shoes, paper,
machine tools, graphics) by science-based industries (chemical and petrochemical, electronic, information-processing) represented one of the last
half-century's major themes of technological innovation. The science-based industries pre-empted
markets. They served as carriers of new technological systems. In the forties, for example, the
chemical industry's invasion of textiles yielded synthetic fibers and finishes, and in the fifties virtually
the entire range of new textile products based on
synthetics. The effect was to lock clusters of industries together. New industrial complexes have made
the Standard Industrial Classification Manual obsolete. Now we have not a textile industry, but a
textile-chemical-paper complex; not a machine

tool industry, but a 'materials-forming' industry. And individual firms have had to incorporate the elements of diverse technologies and businesses associated with these new definitions of industries. A major textile manufacturer has synthetic fiber, non-woven, and information-processing divisions. A large machine tool builder has divisions for plastics, precision-forging, chemical-forming and numerically controlled machine tools.

◆ *Research- and development-based companies worked out the logical consequences of the concept of technological innovation as an inherent business function.* A large appliance company, heavily engaged in the manufacture of refrigerators, developed a new method of food preservation. The method depended on the use of burners to control the concentration of oxygen and CO_2 in a closed chamber. Although the method produced impressive laboratory results, the firm rejected it: it offered no inducements to an enterprise that already controlled one-third of the US refrigerator market; if anything, the new method threatened to disrupt profitable established systems for distributing and merchandising refrigerators.

But the developers of the method were unwilling to give it up. They thought of using the burners to prolong the life of fruits and vegetables in storage —an achievement which would allow farmers to hold their produce while they waited for the most favorable market. They commissioned a piece of market research—and went along to make sure that it came out right. They persuaded the corporate president (whose father had been one of the inventors of the telephone) to establish an autonomous subsidiary to market the device, and they joined the new company as heads of marketing and research.

3M (Minnesota Mining and Manufacturing) began by making minerals. They ground up the minerals and deposited them on a substrate with glue and cut it into pieces and had sandpaper. Sandpaper was their classical business product. Around World War II a man named Cooke in their research department invented a tape which was transparent and which you could stick on things. He called it Scotch tape. The idea was that you were supposed to save money with it. You could mend books instead of throwing them away. But in fact, when they put Scotch tape on the market, they discovered quite differently. What do you do with Scotch tape? How do you use it? Well, you wrap up presents with it, you hang things on the wall. My teenage daughter fixes her hair with it. It turns out that Scotch tape is a projective test for consumers. And the 3M company has a marketing style that is beautifully adapted to that. They have now come up with hair-fixing Scotch tape, noticing what consumers have done. 3M in that sense has become a learning system.

All of these trends have combined to effect certain major shifts. In response to new technologies, industrial invasions and diversification away from saturated markets, *the firm has tended to evolve from a pyramid, built around a single relatively static product line, to a constellation of semi-autonomous divisions.*

The constellation firm can no longer be defined in terms of a class of products—however general the class may be. There is no set of properties which all and only the products of the firm possess. Instead, the products of the firm bear to one another a family resemblance, which reflects the processes of development through which one led to another.

The firm defines itself as the vehicle for carrying out a

special kind of *process*. It defines itself through its engagement in entrepreneurship, the launching of new ventures, or in commercializing what comes out of development.

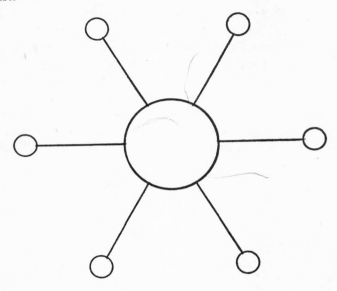

The constellation firm displays peculiar capabilities for adaptation. Each semi-autonomous unit may be discarded when it gets into trouble, and new units brought into being, without disturbing the other units and without requiring major shifts in the nucleus of the firm.

The principal figure in the firm becomes the manager of the corporate entrepreneurial process; and the central planning question is this: 'What are the potentials in development for new commercial ventures?'

From products to business systems

In the business firm's evolution over the last half-century, while the firm has acquired the capacity to diffuse whole industries and in some cases to sustain technological innovation within them, it has always defined itself around its product. At the present time, however, products are becoming obsolete. This is not to say merely that particular products are obsolescent, but that we are evolving away from the product as the unit around which business organizations are defined and towards integration around 'business systems'.

The potency of the concept of business systems owes a great deal to the aerospace and weapons systems of the last thirty years. NASA, for example, cannot be said to be in any traditional sense an industry. It is an immense organization, made up of government agencies, laboratories, and related contractors, all devoted (until recently) to the aim of getting man to the moon. NASA's organization reflects this aim.

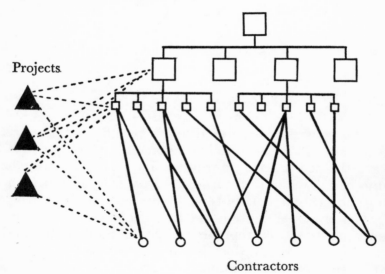

Projects

Contractors

An administrator, together with associate administrators, oversees the central components of NASA's major functions: mission-operations, management of laboratories, organization and administration. A project organization cuts across this basic administrative arrangement. Each project has its own sub-objective and an array of organizational components responsible for functions associated with that sub-objective—for example, propulsion systems, communications, guidance, life support. The project manager's task is to coordinate the complex of government agencies, laboratories, and contractors involved in performance of these functions. NASA's total budget for the performance of these functions has been of the order of $5 billion a year.

Contrast the manner in which the nation carries out another major function, which might be described as 'keeping us in clean clothes'.

The main thing about *this* function is that no person or agency is responsible for it. It is carried out through the interaction of elements of what are usually considered separate industries:

- The 'chain' of linked textile industries spins yarn from fiber or filament; makes, cuts and converts cloth; and manufactures, distributes and markets apparel.

- The soap and chemical complex manufactures, distributes and markets soaps, solvents, detergents and other cleaning materials.

- The appliance complex manufactures and distributes commercial and domestic equipment for laundering and cleaning garments.

- The service industry consists of laundering and dry-cleaning establishments.

- Consumers wear clothes, have them cleaned, and themselves perform many of the tasks of maintenance and cleaning.

This is an oversimple description. Nevertheless, the relations among its elements already appear to be extremely complex.

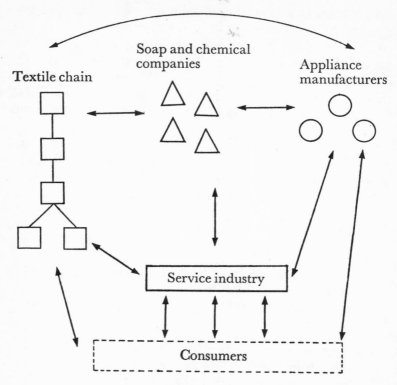

Fiber and apparel manufacturers produce the garments which are to be cleaned in the machines made by appliance makers, using materials produced by soap and chemical makers, in operations frequently carried out by consumers. When the process fails to work properly, it is hard to fix responsibility. With the proliferation of new fibers and finishes in the fifties, there was considerable confusion over what sorts of garments were to be cleaned, under what conditions, with what sorts of cleaning materials. Appliance manufacturers blamed the textile industry for failing to adopt a clear and uniform labelling system. Textile manufacturers blamed appliance and chemical companies for failing to adapt their products to the demands of the new fabrics. And all of them, at various times, blamed the consumer for lack of intelligence.

This complex of industries, organizations and institutions, all subsumed under the function of 'keeping us in clean clothes', we will call a business system. Any complex of firms related to one another in the performance of a major social function is a business system. On this particular business system the nation spends about $5 billion per year.

Within the system, 'innovation' turns out frequently to be a response, at a lag, in one part of the system to what another part of the system has done.

◆ In 1960 a group of consultants proposed to the Whirlpool Corporation that they produce a 'solvent washer' which would be, in effect, a home dry-cleaning machine for all kinds of garments. Whirlpool, it turned out, already had a version of the idea. But its market studies had convinced it that women would resist any increase in the amount of ironing they had to do; home dry-cleaners would simply produce more clothes to be ironed.

In the early sixties, however, 'wash-and-wear' gained acceptance. And wash-and-wear fabrics could in most cases be 'finished' acceptably without ironing. The introduction of wash-and-wear released the idea of the coin-operated dry-cleaner, which had been on Whirlpool's shelves. Norge had the same ideal. And Whirlpool and Norge raced to be first to the market with the 'coin-ops'.

The introduction of the coin-ops confronted traditional private dry-cleaning establishments with a new form of competition. The result was to force such companies either to set up 'coin-op' concessions, to turn themselves into more industrialized dry-cleaning establishments better able to meet the new competition, or to specialize in 'craft' work highly geared to the needs of particular customers, so that in special areas they could outperform the 'coin-ops'.

In the meantime, people were cleaning their clothes in common equipment at room temperature. Bacterial problems arose which created the 'need' for new bacteriostats that could function effectively in 'coin-ops'.

The business system as a whole had been significantly transformed, but through a kind of systems-interaction managed by no one. An innovation in one part of the system had led to another, creating waves of new requirements to which others in the system had to respond in still different ways. To each element in the system, the wave brought requirements or opportunities for new products and services. The diffusion of product-innovation contributed to an overall transformation of the system whose character became clear only after the fact.

It is a sign of the times, however, that in California new firms engage in 'keeping customers in clean shirts'. They are neither cleaning establishments, shirt manufacturers, retailers, nor manufacturers of cleaning equipment. They contract to keep their customers regularly supplied with clean shirts, meeting specifications of size, color, style and cleanliness. They control, either by ownership or by contractual arrangement, sources of shirt manufacture as well as cleaning establishments. They retain the decision to supply the customer with a new shirt or to launder his old one. They retain control of the decision to 'make or buy'. And they control enough of the elements of the business system (at least as it applies to shirts) to be able to manage system-wide innovations—for example, to introduce new cleaning methods to accommodate new kinds of fabric. Such a firm defines and organizes itself not around any product, but around a business system.

What emerges is a new strategy of growth. In the thirties, forties and fifties, businesses grew through 'horizontal' or 'vertical' integration. In horizontal integration, one firm acquired or established other firms engaged in similar processes of manufacture and marketing. It replicated the classical business firm, expanded it, gave it a more nearly secure position in its market, and permitted it economies of scale in purchasing, the use of manpower, the costs of marketing and the like. Vertical integration put under single corporate control more links in the manufacturing-marketing chain. Papermaking firms, for example, came to control their own woodlands as well as plants for processing the timber and for manufacturing and marketing the end-product. When a firm placed these vertical elements of the system under single corporate control, it made possible a more effective balancing of supply and demand for each intermediate operation, a reduction of costs through elimination of 'middle man' profits, and a tailoring of each intermediate operation to the changing needs of operations further down the ladder.

The vertical and horizontal integration of firms received its impetus from the pressures and opportunities for business growth: the expansion of markets, the increasing availability of capital, the transition from family to public ownership and from family to professional management. The industrial giants of the thirties and forties—the great steel, paper, automotive and chemical companies, for example—assumed this form. They aggregated and compressed similar product-centered firms and the business links which connected them, on the one hand, to sources of supply and, on the other, to end-users. But throughout this process, the classical definition and organization of industries remained very much intact.

But the 'business system firm' has a kind of integration which is neither 'horizontal' nor 'vertical'. It takes different 'cuts' at business systems: it integrates a mix of the elements of a business system—elements which are neither horizontally nor vertically related to one another but which combine to perform a major social function. That is, it neither combines companies manufacturing similar end products nor links together the chains of companies that connect raw materials to consumer goods, but organizes sets of product and service companies that interact to make up a business system.

◆   Firms have grown up around 'institutional feeding'. They take on the function of providing meals to specification for certain numbers of people in certain institutions (hospitals, schools, airliners, hotels). They control not only the purchasing of raw materials, the preparation of intermediates, and the final preparation, but the design and manufacture of equipment, utensils, and maintenance equipment. They may be integrated back to agriculture, if that seems desirable, or to the steel in their forks. They retain, at each point, the freedom to decide to make or buy, own or franchise, employ one supplier or a number.

Such a firm stands an excellent chance of orchestrating the various innovations required to transform the feeding system. If the economic use of infra-red ovens depends, for example, on the uniform slicing of meat to certain thicknesses, the firm can assure that uniformity.

◆   In New York, a new firm combines a dredging service for New York harbor with a land development firm. The product of the dredging will provide fill for made land to be developed at the harbor's edge.

◆   Firms organize around service functions—for example, geriatric care. The 'business' consists in the design, development and construction of chains of nursing homes; the recruitment and training of personnel; the design and management of systems for feeding, hygiene, medical care.

◆ A Danish pastor builds a business around a 're-creation system'. A travel service provides customers for a chain of hotels and restaurants dotted throughout Europe; bus and airline companies convey travellers from Denmark to these resorts and back; and a central computer-based information system makes reservations, projects demand, schedules trips, calculates costs. Control over *each* of these elements allows one to serve as customer for the other, permits full utilization of facilities, reduces costs—and leads, in turn, to increased demand.

◆ RCA in Italy operates an 'entertainment system' whose elements include: a 'managing firm' which holds contracts for musicians and artists and manages their careers; recording studios; record and tape companies; chains of retail shops for records and tapes; a television station; a firm specializing in installing stereophonic tape recorders in automobiles.

The movement toward business systems further erodes the boundaries between private and public enterprise. Firms that have come to identify themselves with broad social functions ('providing shelter', 'feeding') have the capability to carry out functions usually reserved for public institutions.

In part, this reflects the growing market for public systems such as housing, transportation, waste management and the like. In part, it reflects recognition that, if a new technology is to be introduced into a public system, the whole system must be restructured.

◆   In the decade between 1950 and 1960, ten American firms invested well over $1 million each in the design and development of 'housing systems'. Monsanto, Koppers, Alcoa, Johns Manville, among others, had examined the growing housing market and its projected future growth as a percentage of gross national product. They had observed, as well, that many of the elements of cost in a house—particularly the high cost of labor—seemed to derive from the fact that a house is assembled, largely by craft, out of a conglomeration of products. What if houses were designed, produced and marketed as industrial systems?

Each company invested in the development of a housing system which would employ its own products—Monsanto, plastics; Koppers, polystyrene foam; Alcoa, aluminium. The Koppers house, for example, consisted of plywood-polystyrene 'skin structure' sandwiches, fastened together with wooden splines. The components could be manufactured efficiently and cheaply in a factory and assembled on site with relatively little labor. But each company discovered independently that 'public systems' are also a plenum, in which prevailing technologies link to dynamically conservative social systems.

Specifically, these industrial firms discovered that housing falls under the jurisdiction of approximately 2,000 separate municipal building codes, each of which is supported by the complex of institutions (craft labor unions, code inspectors, building material suppliers). It may be possible to persuade code inspectors in Duluth of the acceptability of the Koppers system, but the battle must be fought again in Cedar Rapids and again in Kansas City. Soon the cost of marketing exceeds even the most optimistic estimate of profits.

Public systems, then, like business systems, are dynamically conservative social and intellectual systems built around prevailing technology. The established system will resist any significant technological innovation. A significant technological innovation will fail in a situation favorable to the introduction of a new *system* unless the other complementary components of the system can be made available.

◆ Firms like Raytheon, General Learning, and Xerox have organized divisions around 'educational systems' and claim the capability for initiating and managing all of the functions associated with an educational objective—for example, planning the junior college system of a community, developing curriculum and materials, training and recruiting teachers, and overseeing the construction of buildings.

◆ Westinghouse and Walt Disney Productions have entered the 'city business', which means that they have defined whole communities as their units of development and, beginning with land speculation, they are prepared to undertake land improvement, road-building, housing developments, construction of schools and community facilities, preparation of industrial sites and attraction of industry.

◆ Litton Industries and Corn Products Corporation have taken on, in developing countries, programs of agricultural and industrial development of a breadth usually associated only with big government. CPC, for example, is engaged in one Latin American country in performing a set of functions analogous to the work of the Agriculture Department in the United States—introduction of new crop varieties and methods, construction of 'packaged' food-processing plants, training of farmers, provision of technical assistance.

Such firms have under their control the elements required to permit the transformation of whole systems. If a firm controls the nature of the equipment to be used in preparing the food for its market, it can afford to introduce foods which need special preparation. If the firm can figure out how to modify or replace its preparation equipment economically, it need not wait for complementary innovation on the part of another element of the system, nor does it have to rely on persuasion. But the investments required to permit systems-wide control must be justified by the volume and profitability of the new forms of business to be generated.

The firm has internalized those elements of the business system (and the relationships between them) which would otherwise be split between separate industries and corporations. The firm gains capability, therefore, for initiating and managing the innovation and diffusion, not of products or techniques alone, but of whole new systems related to its central function.

The management of a business systems firm poses special problems, and it is not surprising that some firms seeking to organize around complex business systems have encountered major difficulties. For such a firm, 'management' now means the creation and maintenance of a network of components inside the firm which would have been handled through a variety of transactions with outside institutions. Changes of investment in one component produce chain reaction among others. Innovations in any one area penetrate all areas. The system must become capable of planning for all components in a balanced and comprehensive way, and its internal network of information and control must be adequate to detect and modulate events in one area which have significant implications for the system as a whole. As a diffusion system, the firm must take into account, and generate in each wave of expansion, all the elements required for the performance of the system's function. It cannot make decisions about expansion merely on the basis of an assumed market for its product. It cannot introduce a new product and let things take care of themselves. In order to make such decisions, it must assess the adequacy of a given functional system in a region, the problems associated with the introduction of a new system for performing that function, and the firm's own resources for carrying out that introduction—including the resulting dislocation of established firms and workers.

The firm has no stable base in the technologies of particular products or the systems built around them. It is, therefore, an internal learning system in which the system's interactions, illustrated by the example of the 'coin-op' dry-cleaner, must now become a matter of directed transformation of the whole system. These directed transformations are in part the justification for the business systems firm. But they oblige it to internalize processes of information flow and sequential innovation which have traditionally been left to the 'market' and to the chain reactions within and across industry lines— reactions in which each firm had only to worry about its own response as one component. The business firm, representing the entire functional system, must now learn to effect the transformation and diffusion of the system as a whole.

4 Diffusion of innovation

When we speak of 'the formation of social policy', we envisage society as a giant 'decider' and we see social change as a process in which society confronts its changing situation, makes up its mind what is to be done, and carries out its decisions.

There is an entirely different perspective on social change—one shared by anthropologists, economists and students of the history of technology, as well as by some business managers—according to which social change occurs as inventions come into use and fan out over the society. Here, the central metaphor is not 'deciding' but 'spread', 'propagation', or 'contagion'. Diffusion of innovation is a dominant model for the transformation of societies according to which novelty moves out from one or more points to permeate the society as a whole.

Systems for diffusion are critical to the learning capacity of a society. They evolve over time. Their evolution tends to follow changing infrastructure technology —technology for the flows of men, materials, money and information. Theories of diffusion tend to be based on old systems; they lag behind our own expanding competence. They fail, therefore, as guides for policy and action now, but they are remarkably stubborn and resilient.

In what follows, I will examine evolving models for the diffusion of innovations, make explicit some of the assumptions on which they rest, and hold them up against recent experience.

The center-periphery model

Those who have tried to account for social change via the diffusion of innovations, and those who have sought to develop and promote new systems for diffusion (most notably, in agriculture, medicine, and industrial development) have relied heavily upon the center-periphery model.

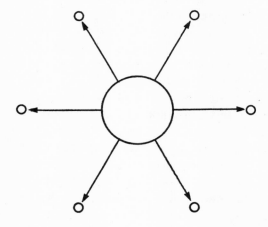

This model rests on three basic elements:

♦ The innovation to be diffused exists, fully realized in its essentials, prior to its diffusion.

♦ Diffusion is the movement of an innovation from a center out to its ultimate users.

♦ Directed diffusion is a centrally managed process of dissemination, training, and provision of resources and incentives.

Advocates of center-periphery theory have tended to see diffusion as 'the human interaction in which one person communicates a new idea to another person. Thus, at its most elemental level of conceptualization, the diffusion process consists of (1) a new idea, (2) individual A who knows about the innovation, and (3) individual B who does not know about the innovation. . . .'[1] The prototype of the 'diffuser' is the agricultural extension agent, the medical 'detail man' (who introduces new pharmaceuticals to doctors), salesmen, nurses and doctors, school administrators and teachers. Diffusion studies tend to focus on products or techniques like new plant varieties, weed sprays, insecticides, drugs, and public health practices. But the dominant model remains the US Agricultural Extension program whose perceived success in increasing agricultural productivity in the late nineteenth and early twentieth centuries has made it a paradigm for all later students of directed diffusion.

The effectiveness of a center-periphery system depends first upon the level of resources and energy at the center, then upon the number of points at the periphery, the length of the radii or spokes through which diffusion takes place, and the energy required to gain a new adoption. The diffusion capability of an agricultural extension agent, for example, depends upon his own energies and skills, the number and location of the farmers he serves, and the time and effort he must devote to work with each farmer.

Scope depends, as well, on infrastructure technology. The scope of the center-periphery system varies directly with the level of technology governing the flows of men, materials, money and information. Public health officials, who try to spread new methods of birth control in India, use elephants to reach thousands of small villages over roads difficult to pass at any time and impossible in certain seasons. The use of elephants reflects not only a solution to the transportation problem but an ingenious sense of public relations.

Finally, the scope of a center-periphery system depends on its capacity for generating and managing feedback. Because the process of diffusion is originally regulated by the center, the effectiveness of the process depends upon the ways in which information moves from the periphery back to the center.

There are two important variants to the center-periphery model:

- *'Johnny Appleseed'* Here the primary center is a kind of bard who roams his territory spreading a new message. Into this category fall the traveling scholars, saints and artisans of the Middle Ages; Voltaire and Thomas Paine; and contemporary bards of radical activism like Saul Alinsky.

- *The 'magnet' model* The 'magnet' attracts agents of diffusion to it, as universities have long since done. With the flowering of science and medicine in the universities of nineteenth-century Germany, for example, students flocked to Germany from all parts of the world and then returned to their own country to teach and practice what they had learned. The United States, Britain and the Soviet Union play magnet, particularly in technology and economics, to developing nations.

The magnet model offers advantages. It permits tighter control of the teaching and greater efficiency in the use of teachers. But it has less control over what happens afterwards, and permits less variation of doctrine to suit the specialized needs of the outposts.

The Johnny Appleseed model allows the teaching to be adapted to the special conditions of the territories. But there is less opportunity for the development of a critical mass at the center capable of attracting new adherents.

The traveling center or the magnet center may spawn new centers. But in neither case does it monitor or manage the process of dissemination. Once the new centers are established, for better or worse, they pursue their disparate paths.

When the center-periphery system exceeds the resources or the energy at the center, overloads the capacity
of the radii, or mishandles feedback from the periphery,
it fails. Failure takes the form of simple ineffectiveness in
diffusion, distortion of the message, or disintegration of
the system as a whole.

Detail men working for a drug company communicate
with doctors in their territory. When they have insufficient time to reach their quota of doctors, they may reduce their level of effort with each doctor to a point where
they are unable to convey the company's message effectively. Or they may lose contact with their own central
office, garbling new messages. If, as a result, sales fall off
and salesmen lose morale, the system as a whole may fall
apart.

The proliferation of centers

This is an elaboration of the center-periphery model, designed as though to extend the limits and overcome the
sources of failure inherent in the simpler model.

This system retains the basic center-periphery structure, but differentiates primary from secondary centers.

Secondary centers engage in the diffusion of innovations; primary centers support and manage secondary centers. The effect is to multiply many-fold the reach and efficiency of the diffusion system. The system's scope still depends both on the level of energy and resources at the center, and on infrastructure technology. But there is an exponential increase in the leverage of a given central resource and a given state of infrastructure technology. Each secondary center now has the scope of what would have been the whole system. The limits to the reach and effectiveness of the new system depend now on the primary center's ability to generate, support and manage the new centers.

The model of the proliferation of centers has had many prototypes, but among the first and most important was the Roman army. The army's advance guard moved out from Rome to invade new territories, subjugate peoples and establish colonies. The business of the outposts was war and government. As a corollary to subjugation, each outpost established in its territory an approximation to the Roman way of life. There was a centrally established doctrine and a centrally established method for diffusing it. Each outpost functioned as a center of control and diffusion, linked to the primary center in Rome.

Among the early Christian missionaries there was a central, pre-established doctrine and a fixed methodology for its dissemination. In the more elaborate and disciplined missionary systems like the sixteenth century Jesuit organization of Ignatius Loyola, a highly disciplined nuclear band, indoctrinated both in Catholic religion and in technique for its diffusion, sent emissaries throughout the world. In this society for the propagation of the faith each emissary functioned as a center of teaching and diffusion. The central office trained, deployed and managed these agents of change.

The model of the proliferation of centers makes of the primary center a trainer of trainers. The central message includes not only the content of the innovation to be diffused, but a pre-established method for its diffusion. The primary center now specializes in training, deployment, support, monitoring and management. And the new specialization purchases an exponential increase in effectiveness.

The missionary model resembles the model of colonization. Perhaps it is no accident that colonization of the New World, from the sixteenth century on, allied itself with missionary activity. In the colonial model it is an entire way of life that is diffused. Colonists move out from a mother country from which they are monitored, supported and managed. Their diffusion proceeds only secondarily by communicating innovations to others, and primarily by an expansion of the agents of diffusion into their surrounding environments.

The late nineteenth and early twentieth centuries were marked by the flowering of a cluster of highly developed models along the lines of the proliferation of centers:

◆ Industrial expansion

◆ The Communist movement

◆ Imperialism.

All were characterized by highly specialized primary centers and by the exploitation of the new infrastructure technologies of steam and rail for the maintenance of the network of primary and secondary centers. As distinguished from the models of the magnet and Johnny Appleseed, systems for the management and control of secondary centers became predominant.

Industrial expansion came about on a world-wide scale through a form of specialization reminiscent of the Roman army. The central message now took the form of technology both for production and for the management of the business firm. These spread throughout the world as industrial centers established decentralized networks of distribution, marketing, production, manpower and financial control.

The patterns have been varied. Agents of the central firm established new centers throughout the target territories, replicating the central methods of the industry. Or they took over existing decentralized operations and subjugated them to central control. In some cases the firm decentralized whole industrial systems. In other cases it decentralized marketing and distribution and kept production central. The story of the variations is the story of the growth of modern industrial enterprise.

Cutting across all variants, however, there is a dominant pattern in the primary center's relationship to secondary centers:

♦ The primary center is a guardian of pre-established doctrine and methodology.

♦ It selects territories for expansion, and deploys and organizes agents of expansion.

♦ It is not only the source and model of operations to be diffused but the developer of methodologies for diffusion.

♦ It trains and incubates new agents of diffusion.

♦ It supports decentralized outposts through capital, information and know-how.

♦ It monitors and manages decentralized operations, setting criteria for performance, monitoring performance, observing and overseeing leadership in the outposts.

♦ It maintains information throughout the network of outposts.

The Coca Cola company is a later model of the type. It functions on a world-wide basis. It has established a name and a product, as well as a method of operation, which permits it to replicate again and again a single system for production, distribution and marketing. The simplicity and uniformity of its central message permits a system of deployment and control capable of encompassing the world as a whole.

The Communist movement   In the early decades of the twentieth century, Communism produced a system of diffusion which rivaled industrial expansion in scope and design. It had a fixed doctrine for dissemination, an established methodology for diffusion, and an international system of cells.

The functions of the center are comparable:

◆   The management of the overall movement

◆   The training of leaders for the cells

◆   Control over the cells through central policy and the maintenance of rewards and punishments

◆   The monitoring and replacement of leadership

◆   Provision of a model for imitation on the part of the cells

◆   Progressive maintenance of the central doctrine and of the methodology for its diffusion

◆   Management of the overall network of cells.

The system had special features. Its message was one of economic, social and political revolution, and revolution was its strategy of diffusion. But the center of diffusion was also a nation. The dissemination of revolutionary doctrine mingled with a struggle for national hegemony.

Imperialism   Nineteenth century imperialism succeeded European colonialism and consisted not only in colonization but in the economic and political domination of colonial peoples. The strategy of empire was one of military domination, followed by military occupation and then by civilian colonial government. Most frequently, imperial government meant extraction of the nation's raw materials in the interests of the mother country. But it meant, as well, the imposition of the mother country's way of life on the colonial nation. Institutions were exported wholesale and an imperial elite served as a model for subjugated nations, creating both pressures and incentives for adopting the way of life represented by the mother country.

Great Britain's pattern was more widespread and in some ways more impressive than those of other European nations, but the contents of these patterns were basically similar. Great Britain established colonial governments in Africa, Asia, and the Middle East. Commerce and military conquest led to military government and then to the simulacrum of civilian government along the lines of the British model. British civil servants entered the country to create remarkably stable bureaucracies. The British influence permeated the country's institutions in religion, education, business, trade, military organization and even sport. British agents and colonists were both manipulators and models for colonial peoples. And Britain itself became a magnet training ground for them. All of this was in the name of military and economic advantage. Under the ideology of empire, the diffusion of the British way of life was a by-product of the search for advantage.

Not surprisingly, these diffusion systems came to be confused with one another. Critics have seen Communism as a form of imperialism. Historians have described both Communism and imperialism as vehicles for industrial expansion. Perhaps all three were variants of a central process of world-wide westernization, industrialization or modernization.

Why did these variant models develop at about the same time? To answer, we would need to examine the role of the new infrastructure technology of steam and rail and the flowering of industrial production technology.

Both had the effect of making the world into 'territory'. We would have to consider the power of the metaphors of the machine and of early biological theories of cell formation and reproduction.

The forms of failure

When the model of the proliferation of centers fails, the secondary centers get out of control. In missionary organizations this takes the form of heresy; in colonialism, revolution: in Communism, deviationism. In industrial organization, failure takes the form of fragmentation, insubordination, and the classical problems of center-branch conflict.

But what looks like heresy or deviationism from the point of view of central, may look to the secondary center like innovation appropriate to its region. In this context we can understand the conflicts of colonial outposts with the mother country and the familiar complaints of regional offices that central is unresponsive and out of touch with local problems.

When secondary centers get disconnected from central, the diffusion system fragments and becomes unable to maintain itself and expand. It may still transform dispersed societies. But the transformation no longer consists in diffusion of an established message. It leads, rather, to a variety of regional transformations which bear only a family resemblance to one another.

In failure, the model of the proliferation of centers may become a learning system in spite of itself. But it is a learning system in which the feedback loop is not from secondary to primary centers, but from secondary centers to themselves.

The process as a whole, then, has a pattern something like the following:

1 A primary center emerges.

2 It develops a diffusion system.

The primary center replicates itself in many secondary centers.

The primary center specializes in creation and management of secondary centers and in maintenance of the overall network.

3 The diffusion system fragments.

Central loses control.

The network disintegrates.

Secondary centers gain independence (*or* they decline, *or* one of them assumes the role of primary center.)

Sources of failure

These are variants of the same conditions that lead to failure in the simple center-periphery model.

The limits of infrastructure When the network of communications of money, men, information and materials is inadequate to the demands imposed on it, the system must either retrench or fail. The far greater scope of the model of proliferation of centers depends on a more advanced infrastructure technology (specifically, on the technologies of transportation and communication developed in the late nineteenth and early twentieth centuries). But the need for rapid central response, or for a more differentiated response to widely varying regional conditions, may overtax the available infrastructure. Or the introduction of new infrastructure technology may disrupt a relatively stable diffusion system.

Constraints on the resources of the center The demands on leadership and management may overwhelm the system as the primary center takes on new responsibilities. The new functions of training, selecting territories and nurturing leadership create problems of balance between the needs for central direction and for attention to special regional problems. Competence in creating networks differs from competence in maintaining them. The transition from one to the other is difficult. There is a tendency to underestimate the *difference* between these kinds of competence and the kinds of competence required by the secondary centers themselves.

The motivation of the agent of diffusion   In the model of the proliferation of centers, the agent of diffusion is of two kinds, the field man who makes first contact and first communicates the central message, and the local or regional entrepreneur who builds up regional centers. The latter are the heads of mission, branch managers, local governors and cell leaders. Their situation, particularly in the early stages, may be something like this:

◆   The environment is always foreign and often hostile. The agents confront local resistances and dangers that central can never know as intensively as they, and that central may ignore altogether. Central always seems to be out of contact and slow in response. The central message may appear strange and inappropriate in the new setting. There are often strong local counter-pressures threatening to engulf the mission. The mission, moreover, feels alienated from the center of power—where policy is being made and where battles for power are going on. This distance from the center can be agonizing when there is uncertainty over change of direction at central, or when central seems simply unresponsive to local requirements.

What moves an agent of diffusion to enter a situation like this may be a desire for new territory, attraction to adventure and romance, flight from an intolerable situation at center, or—perhaps most importantly—a religious attachment to the central message. This 'missionary mentality' may attach itself to empire, to revolution or even to Coca Cola. The more threatening the local system, the more tenuous the contact with central, the more congenial the situation to the missionary—providing the central message remains capable of sustaining its religious burden.

Regional diversity and the rigidity of central doctrine   Territories are different from one another and from central. Does the central message lend itself to modification to take account of regional differences? What are the limits of acceptable deviation? Does the feedback loop between central and the regions permit modification of the central message?

In the Communist Internationale, party-liners came into conflict with partisans who believed in the right of each country to find its own road to revolution. Failure may occur in industrial expansion out of central's insistence on its way of doing business without taking into account the special features of local situations—for example, the special problems created for Coca Cola by the unique demands of the African market or the problems created for the Corn Products Company by the special requirements of agribusiness in Latin America. A colonial administration may fail by refusing to recognize and build on local institutions, such as the institutions of the chief and witchcraft in African tribal societies.

Similar problems of rigidity hold for the *method* to be used in diffusion. There is as much conflict between regional and central over this as over the message to be diffused. Consider, for example, the conflicts between the central business office and regional branches over marketing methods, or the conflict between regional outposts and central offices over methods of diffusing techniques of birth-control.

Resolution of these kinds of conflict may be achieved through central's ability to alter its message in response to local needs. Or the diffusion system may avert the conflicts altogether by adopting a central message which is like a kind of constitution, in the sense that it provides guidance for action and yet lends itself to variations without 'breaking'. In either case, the set of secondary centers comes to look more like a family of overlapping and analogous situations than like a set of replications of a single model.

Normative use of the model

The center-periphery model, with its extension in the form of the proliferation of centers, is not only historically important.[2] It has also become the dominant normative model for diffusion.

Agricultural development programs in Africa and Latin America, for example, draw on the model of successful agricultural extension programs in the United States. The model requires centers of technological competence like experimental stations, model farms, central laboratories, land grant universities, and experts in technical assistance, who communicate the new technologies of agriculture to the farmers in their territories.

In the field of medicine and health care, a major current program rests on the concept of local 'centers of excellence' (medical research and teaching centers) whose purpose is to communicate the new medical technology to peripheral rings of community physicians. The assumption is that the relevant expertise is to be found at the center and communicated to the periphery through new systems for referring patients from one physician to another, training programs, demonstrations, short courses and the like.

When directed diffusion of innovation is at issue, the center-periphery model is simply what comes to mind. But a normative theory of diffusion based on the center-periphery model has inadequacies beyond the historical failings of actual center-periphery systems. In two crucial respects, the prevailing theories fail to take into account phenomena underlying some of their successes.

Diffusion as communication   Everett Rogers, who simply reflects current thinking on the subject, treats the act of diffusion as an act of communication: 'The essence of the diffusion process is the human interaction in which one person communicates a new idea to a new person.'[3]

The essential process is getting information out, 'communication from A who knows about the innovation to B who does not'. This concept leaves out of account the dynamically conservative plenum into which information moves. The process is more nearly a battle than a communication—a fact recognized, in spite of their failings, by the great nineteenth century models of the proliferation of centers.

Product or technique as the unit of diffusion   Every social system has prevailing technologies and related theories around which it is organically built. Innovation in any aspect of the system threatens the system as a whole. The more significant innovations are those whose acceptance would require more radical transformation of the system; hence their threat to the system is greater.

Rogers, along with other exponents of center-periphery theory, considers the diffusion only of new products or techniques which presuppose a relatively stable technological system of which they are components.

A new weed-killer, for example, moves into a system of agricultural technology which includes mechanical plowing, harvesting and spraying, the use of new genetic varieties, chemical fertilizer, crop rotation, mechanical packing equipment, and motorized transportation of crops. Within such a technological system, middle- to large-sized farms are dominant. The economic constraints on farming, as well as the impact of previous technological innovations, have already sharply reduced available farm labor. The acceptance of a new weed-killer depends on equipment which would permit its use over relatively large areas with relatively little labor.

If the weed-killer could be shown to be relatively

effective and innocuous in its side-effects, and if it promised an increase in land productivity or a further reduction in farm labor, then managers of middle- to large-sized farms might accept it fairly readily. Its diffusion might then very well consist of disseminating information, conducting trials, influencing opinion leaders, and the like. But this would be because the weed-killer meshes with a pre-existing technological system whose objectives it seems likely to enhance with relatively little disruption. For that system, it is not, in the sense we have been using the term, a very significant innovation.

The situation is quite different where the introduction of the innovation requires significant disruption of the entire technological-social system and the system of ideas related to it. In such a case, diffusion of an innovation looks less like the dissemination of information than like a sequence of related disruptions of complex systems, resulting in each case in a new configuration. Here the unit of diffusion is not a product or technique but a whole technological system.

Systems as units of diffusion

Where the unit of diffusion is more nearly a complete technological system than a single product or technique, the process involved in the diffusion of significant innovation resembles the generation and diffusion of industries. For purposes of comparison, let us examine the development and diffusion of a new industry—the granite industry in New England in the late eighteenth and early nineteenth centuries.

The industry depended on the geology of the New England region.

Along the northern boundary of the whole back shore area [East Gloucester] lies a prehistoric geological landmark, a long stretch of uncovered terminal moraine. In his classical report on the geology of Cape Ann, Professor Shaler stated that the terminal moraine occupies about three-quarters of the area of Cape Ann east of the Annisquam River. It is evidenced by the boulders on Dogtown and elsewhere. But only on the ridge north of East Gloucester, Joppa, and Beaver Dam is there a long uncovered stretch.[4]

From earliest colonial times, surface granite, in the form of boulders, had been put to limited use.

After the first settlers came to Boston, they probably found the land upon which the city now stands covered with an abundant supply of New England boulders, which were at once useful in the construction of buildings, just as they are now used in the country districts, but it seems probable that no ledge of rock was found in the old town. Opinions differ, however, as to this point, for Judge Sewall in his diary mentions getting out building stones from the Common as late as 1693. There was the wishing stone near the junction of Beacon Street mall, and the path leading to Joy Street, and we are told 'the young folks of bygone days used to walk nine times around this stone, and then standing or setting upon it silently make their wishes.'

That they began at once to use stone for houses is shown in the following record: 'October 30, 1630: a stone house which the governor was erecting at Mystic was washed down to the ground in a violent storm, the walls being laid in clay instead of lime.' Mud houses were, indeed, known in the early days of the town, but these were very few in number, and, of course, were only occupied by the poorest of the colonists; or, more correctly speaking, by their menials only. A few houses were built of stone and some of brick, but these were exceptions to the general rule until Boston had become over twenty years of age. About 1650, Johnson says of the city, '. . . the buildings are beautiful and large, some fairly set forth with brick, tile, stone and slate.'[5]

But until the late eighteenth century, there had been no quarrying and no large-scale granite industry.

The first impetus to the development of the granite industry came in the course of the Revolutionary War. Among the German mercenaries the British imported to fight the colonists were many who carried with them the

stone cutter's art as it had been practiced in their home-
land. A group of these settled in New England in a place
which was first named Germantown and later became
Quincy.

> . . . this class of German artisans first introduced into this
> country the practice of preparing hewn or hammered stone,
> wrought to a plain surface, sufficiently straight and smooth
> to make a regular wall. The process as then practiced by them
> and those who were instructed by them was understood to be
> extremely laborious, and, of course, expensive, as the expense
> depended wholly on the amount of labor required for pre-
> paring it. Without describing the process precisely, which I
> do not understand sufficiently to do, I understand the first
> thing to be done was if the rock was in a quarry to blast out
> a portion of it by gunpowder. By this process, fragments
> would come out in all sorts of irregular forms, as by mere
> chance. The business of the workmen then was to take the
> pieces of more regular form and reduce them to smaller and
> more regular shapes, as wanted for building. This is done by
> cutting a groove on a straight line with a hammer made with
> a cutting edge like that of a common axe, then striking it with
> a very heavy beetle on each side of the groove alternately,
> until it would crack generally in the line of such groove.
> This would sometimes split in a line nearly straight,
> though it would often be irregular. In this way, by dividing
> and sub-dividing, the pieces were brought as nearly as prac-
> ticable to the dimensions required, and then all the irregu-
> larities of surface must be removed by hard hewing with very
> heavy instruments.
>
> In this state of the trade, although stone might be gotten
> out and dressed and made suitable for building, yet few
> buildings were erected, probably on account of the great
> expense. . . .[6]

The next phase in the development of the industry cen-
tered around a rather specialized demand.

> Prior to 1798, Castle Island, in Boston Harbor, now Fort
> Independence, was the prison of the State, where convicts
> were sent to be punished by confinement and hard labor.

About that time the United States, in anticipation of hostilities with the French, were desirous of having possession of Castle Island, in order to erect thereon a strong fortification for the defence of Boston, and for that purpose urged on the commonwealth the necessity of having immediate possession of the island. The Commonwealth acceded and caused the prisoners to be removed, although the State Prison, at Charlestown, was not built or ready for their reception, nor was it so for some time after. This fixes the time when the State Prison was in the process of building. Governor Robbins of Milton was one of the first commissioners, and in this capacity put himself into communication with all the workers and dealers in stone and found their prices very uniform, though, as he thought, very high.

Desirous of getting the stone for the prison on the best terms, and believing the prices high, though general, he thought much and conversed much on the subject. In that state of mind, and deeply interested in the subject of stone, he had occasion to pass through Salem in a chaise. In passing along a street he noticed a building apparently new, the basement storey of which was stone. He stopped to look at it carefully. In doing so he perceived along the margin of each stone the marks of a tool at distances of six or seven inches apart. This was something new. He had never seen it on hewn stone. He immediately inquired for the owner and saw him and asked if he knew how and by what process these stones were got out and wrought. He said he did not know, but referred him to the contractor who did most of that species of work in Salem, by the name of Galusha. . . . He then proceeded to find Mr Galusha, and to ask him whether he got out these stones and by what process. He said he did not get them out himself; that they were obtained in Danvers, two or three miles distant, and were furnished by a man named Tarbox.[7]

Samuel Tarbox played a role in the emerging granite industry although he was neither a scientist nor an entrepreneur.

Upon asking for directions to find Mr Tarbox, Governor Robbins was told that he was a very poor man, being in an

obscure situation in Danvers, near the place where the stone
was quarried. Governor Robbins determined to pursue the
inquiry, immediately proceeded to Danvers, and after considerable inquiry, he found Mr Tarbox in a small house with
a family, and with every appearance of poverty about him.[8]

Governor Robbins was explicit in his perception of the
problem as one of directing the diffusion of an essential
innovation.

After some little preliminary conversation, he asked Mr
Tarbox if he got out the stone in question, and if so, his
method. He told him he had, and immediately proceeded to
explain the process, and showed him his tools, his mode of
drilling the holes and inserting and driving the small wedges
as above described.

Governor Robbins was at once struck with the idea that it
was new and peculiar, and might be a very important invention. Governor Robbins did not say that he asked whether it
was an invention of his own, or whether he had learned it of
anybody else. But as it was new to himself, I think he was im-
pressed with the belief that it was the invention of Tarbox. It
did not seem, however, that he had any exclusive or peculiar
interest in the use of his art. Governor Robbins then asked
him if he would consent to go up to Quincy and work two or
three months, and split stone in his mode, so that other workmen might practise it. He said it was impossible for him to
leave home, that his family were dependent on him for their
daily bread, and that he had no clothes suitable to go from
home. Governor Robbins obviated all his objections by
making provisions for the family during his absence, also engaged to give him two or three times the monthly wages
usually paid the best stone cutters, and the man consented.
Having made the necessary arrangements he took him to a
clothing store in Salem, obtained him a suitable outfit, then
took him into his chaise and brought him to Quincy. Governor Robbins added that he introduced Mr Tarbox to several
of the principal stone dealers, and that it was not three
months before every stone-cutter in Quincy could split stones
with small wedges as well as Mr Tarbox. Also that this improvement in the working of granite had in a very short time

the effect to reduce the price to five-eighths of its former cost; that is, that the cost of the dimension stone wanted for the prison, which had before been $4.00, was afterwards reduced to $2.50, and other granite work in similar proportion.[9]

As a consequence, Quincy emerged as a center of the new granite industry.

On Cape Ann, in the meantime, while settlers had long been aware of the granite deposits, there was (in spite of Tarbox's proximity) no quarrying or stone-cutting industry. It was not until 1828 that the convergence of several factors caused a local industry to begin to take shape.

It was a Quincy man, associated with South Shore quarrying operations, who first acted to exploit Cape Ann granite.

The quarry industry got its start on Cape Ann when Nehemiah Knowlton, in 1823, excavated some five hundred tons of stone at Pigeon Cove and advertised it for sale in a Boston newspaper. A Mr Bates of Quincy, where quarries already were in operation, saw the advertisement and came to Pigeon Cove to investigate its resources. He deemed the prospects favorable and began operations there on a ledge which he leased. His venture was not successful, but a couple of years later William Torrey, who had been associated with Mr Bates, opened a pit at another location in Pigeon Cove which became a large quarry. During the next fifteen years he supplied much of the granite used by the federal government in its construction work at Boston and Portsmouth, N.H.[10]

The early granite technology was simple.

When the first quarries were opened, all the work was done by hand-power or ox-power. The holes in which blasting powder was to be exploded were drilled by pounding a square drill with a hammer. Round drills with V-shaped points presently superseded the square drills, but it was not until 1883 that the first steam drill came into use. In the early years, furthermore, the rough slabs of granite were hoisted

out of the pits either by manpower or by oxen, and the pumping of the water which flowed into the pits from the surface
of the ledge or from springs underneath was done by hand. It
was in 1853 that a steam engine was first used for hoisting and
pumping. Late in the nineteenth century numerous mechanical devices were introduced for drilling, cutting, and polishing the granite.[11]

But it set in motion a chain of events which transformed
not only the industry, but the government, the population and the infrastructure of Cape Ann.

From 1700 till after 1820 the settlements at Sandy Bay and
Pigeon Cove increased only slowly in population. Farming,
wood-coasting, and the shore fisheries were the chief occupations of the inhabitants of that period. The harbors on that
section of the Cape were too small and too exposed to the sea
to facilitate an extensive development of the sort of offshore
fishing and foreign trade which took place at Gloucester
Harbor and Annisquam in the eighteenth century.

In 1823, however, a new industry—granite quarrying—
began to develop on a large scale at Pigeon Cove and in
neighboring areas, and that led to such a growth of trade and
such an increase of population that a movement eventually
was started among the residents of Sandy Bay, Pigeon Cove,
and adjoining neighborhoods to have that part of the Cape
separated from Gloucester and set off as an independent
town. As a result, in 1840, by action of the State Legislature,
the town of Rockport came into being. The name 'Rockport'
never had been applied previously to that district; it was
coined for the purpose and chosen by the residents to be the
designation of the new town.[12]

The new industry fed on the rapidly increasing demand
for granite as a building material. And the need to increase output brought a chain of innovations in its wake.

For transporting stone from the quarries to the finishing
sheds and the piers, several quarry companies built inclined
railroad tracks down which the loaded cars traveled by gravity. When empty, they were towed back by oxen. As the
ownership of the quarries became largely connected in the

hands of a few companies, the railroad tracks were extended over a larger area and steam locomotives came into use. The Rockport Granite Company, for example, with quarries both in Pigeon Cove and in Lanesville, operated seven miles of railroad track and three locomotives. . . .[13]

And waves of cheap labor were imported to work the quarries.

Before the days of mechanization, quarrying was a seasonal business, with a curtailment of production during the winter months, and for about twenty-five years after the first quarries were opened, much of the labor was supplied by young men who came to Cape Ann from Maine and New Hampshire for the working season. In the middle of the nineteenth century the quarry industry, like many other New England industries, began to employ immigrant laborers. The first of these were Irish who had left the old country at the time of the potato famine in 1848. They formed a settlement near the quarries, on the outskirts of Lanesville, which was known locally as 'Dublin'.

When the first arrangements for employing Irish immigrants were broached in Pigeon Cove, strong opposition sprang up. 'The house which was being prepared for them to occupy was two or three times blown up with powder; and other means were employed to keep out the unwelcome immigrants.' That opposition undoubtedly was kindled by apprehension that the newcomers would accept employment at wages lower than the rates then being paid.

Immigrants of other nationalities followed the Irish, and in 1875, for example, French Canadian as well as Irish laborers were employed for unskilled work in the quarries at Bay View, and presumably also in Lanesville and Pigeon Cove. English, Scotch, and Irish workmen, as well as Americans, were employed in the more skilled tasks of cutting, finishing, and polishing stone; and a small group of skilled Italian workers was brought in from Genoa for sculpturing the stone to be used for the Boston Post Office, the Myles Standish Monument, and other structures.

About 1880 the quarry companies' continued search for strong-bodied laborers who would work for relatively low

wages led to the bringing in of Finnish immigrants. At first
the Finns were housed in a couple of old barns which had
been converted into dormitories, but they soon established
their families in permanent residences. Thus the population
of Lanesville came to include a large Finnish colony.[14]

By 1860 the Cape's granite industry had reached an impressive scale.

> From those beginnings the industry expanded, both in
> Pigeon Cove and in Lanesville. In 1860, John J. Babson re-
> ported that about 350 men were employed in quarrying the
> stone, in cutting it into the shapes and sizes called for in the
> market, in hauling the stone to the cutters and the shipping
> piers, and in manning the blacksmith shops which were al-
> ways busy sharpening tools and repairing gear. Another 150
> men then were employed on the sloops on which the stone
> was shipped.[15]

It took the beginning of World War I and the introduction of cement as a large-scale building material to initi-
ate the sequence of events which led precipitously to the
industry's decline.

> World War I practically marked the end of the quarry
> industry on Cape Ann. For some years now only one quarry
> has been in operation on the Cape. The industry fell victim
> to technological changes. New and improved methods for the
> manufacture of cement were introduced just before the start
> of World War I, and the labor cost of putting up a building
> with reinforced concrete was so much less than the cost of
> erecting a building with granite blocks that granite construc-
> tion, except for occasional trim, was largely discontinued.
> The rapid increase in the number of automobiles in use,
> which occurred at about the same time, called for smooth
> streets, and the market for paving stones vanished. Thus even
> an industry founded on bedrock could not withstand the
> force of technological change.[16]

The story of the rise and fall of the Cape Ann granite
industry is only one chapter in the industry's diffusion
throughout New England. But that chapter is a micro-

cosm, displaying processes which are common in the diffusion of new industrial systems.

- *The crucial role of war* The industry rose and fell in the interval between two major wars—the Revolutionary War and World War I. The first created the extraordinary conditions of mobility which brought the carriers of stone-cutting technology to the New World. The second set in motion a second revolution in building which displaced the first.

- *The role of the inventor* Tarbox was a prototype of the independent inventor whose contribution triggered the new industry, although he himself was only dimly aware of his own importance and failed to gain any long-term profit from it.

- *The role of pulses of special demand* The new prison of Charlestown sparked Governor Robbins' search, which led to the take-off of the Quincy operation. That operation, in turn, providing a new supply of relatively cheap granite cut to dimension, meshed with and reinforced a growing demand for new fireproof buildings which came with the development of Boston. Thenceforth, the demand and the industry mutually reinforced each other's growth.

- *The interaction of deliberate intervention and unforeseen occurrence* Governor Robbins took on himself the management of a segment of a process of diffusion, when he brought Tarbox to Quincy to teach the local cutters his new method. Entrepreneurs like Torrey, moving out from Quincy, sought deliberately to create new, profitable centers of industry and, in so doing, triggered the industry's spread. The industry's take-off and full development depended on waves of new demand which no one had anticipated or sought deliberately to create.

◆ *The clustering of innovations and the requirements for infrastructure* The growth of the industry in Cape Ann after 1823 depended not only on the new stone-cutting technology but on blasting methods, wire rope and hoisting equipment—and later on steam-powered drills and hoists—which permitted the exploitation of granite in quarries as deep as 500 feet. Requirements for transport drew first on oxen and then on rail technology, and led to the creation of the wharf and the sloop traffic to Boston. The growth of water and rail transport permitted Cape Ann products to travel as far as Washington, DC, and permitted the development of a widespread market whose growth fed into the industry's.

The system of the granite industry grew in interaction with other related systems: the systems of steel, rail transport, steam power, the growing urban systems of the cities of the Atlantic coast, and the migration system, together with its technology, which permitted the entry of successive waves of cheap labor.

No one system caused the others to come into being. Each fed on and reinforced the others. There were precipitating events—the prison, the discovery of Tarbox—but no one of them can be said to have 'caused' the development of the industry. Similarly, individuals and associations intervened at various times and tried, more or less consciously, to forward the industry's diffusion. But no man or group can be said to have directed or managed that diffusion. Each chapter in the diffusion of the granite industry represented a complex reconfiguration of related systems. The development of the industry in Vermont, for example, was analogous but by no means identical to its development at Cape Ann.

Every complex that is in the broadest terms an industry represents just such a socio-technical system as the granite industry on Cape Ann. The agricultural industry, the food industry, the primary metals industry, the nuclear industry, all are systems of technology, production, distribution, marketing, employment and finance. They have developed over time through processes not unlike the one described above. Major non-industrial institutions in our society—institutions for health care, education, and social welfare, for example—represent developing socio-technical systems of a similar kind.

Taken function by function, and (fulfilling these functions) institution by institution, our society represents a dynamically conservative plenum into which innovations must find their way if they are to be diffused. Within such a plenum, potential innovations can be ranked, as we have already suggested, in a kind of target diagram depending on the magnitude of the disruption their acceptance would cause. Innovations lying near the periphery are likely to undergo a diffusion process very much like the ones described by Rogers—a process whose principal features have to do with the dissemination of information, the communication of information from A who knows about the invention to B who does not. But for innovations located near the center of the diagram, which precipitate system-wide changes, the process of diffusion is a battle for broad and complex transformation. And within such a process, the assumptions underlying the classical diffusion model do not hold:

- ◆ The innovation does not by any means entirely antedate the diffusion process; it evolves significantly within that process.

- ◆ The process does not look like the fanning out of innovation from a single source. Many sources of related and reinforcing innovations are likely to be involved.

- ◆ And the process does not consist primarily in centrally managed dissemination of information. This element is usually present, but subordinate to the reorientation of existing socio-technical systems. Deliberate entrepreneurial intervention usually intermeshes with the emergence of new demands comparable in their force to the dynamic conservatism of the established system itself.[17]

Under *these* circumstances, the problem of directed diffusion is to set in motion and guide a chain of related processes of social learning in which sequences of deliberate entrepreneurial intervention interact with unanticipated and inadvertent processes, all more adequately treated under the metaphor of battle than communication.

Recent steps in the evolution of diffusion systems

Theories of diffusion have characteristically lagged behind the reality of emerging systems. The image of the county agent, the detail man and the public health officer still dominate accounts of historical processes of diffusion as they do normative theories of diffusion. Prevailing models of directed diffusion still rest on the great social inventions of the late nineteenth and early twentieth centuries.

As we have seen, these models of directed diffusion do not adequately describe the diffusion systems from which they are derived, when the unit of diffusion is a central rather than a peripheral innovation, or a system as broad as the granite industry.

Even in their reality, moreover, the great nineteenth century proliferation-of-centers systems were inherently limited. They suffered from dependence on limited resources and competence at the primary center, from the rigidity of central doctrine, and from a feedback loop within which information moved primarily between secondary and primary centers. As a consequence, the great institutions for diffusion, such as industry, the church, and world Communism, tend to read their own adaptations as failures of central control.

The development of more nearly adequate theories for the diffusion of innovation must begin by taking account of the existing systems which are already in advance of theories in good currency.

The business firm, as we have seen, evolves toward an advanced learning system. And business firms are very much vehicles for diffusion; marketing is diffusion by another name. Over about the last fifty years, the unit of diffusion around which business firms have organized has evolved from a highly specific product, to a more aggregated product, to constellations of products which bear only a family resemblance to one another, and finally to functional business systems. Concepts of organization, management and planning have evolved along with the unit of diffusion. The business firm, which attained its first great growth through the proliferation of centers, moves toward new models of diffusion as functional systems become central.

During the last decade in which the constellation firm has reached full development and the business systems firm has begun, a very different though in some ways comparable evolution has occurred in domains of society usually considered unrelated or downright antithetical to business. This evolution has followed the pressures for social revolution stemming from a cluster of interrelated movements for civil rights, black power, peace, disarmament and student revolt. These are all national or international causes, but at regional and local levels they have been allied with movements against urban renewal, dislocation of neighborhoods by superhighways and abuses of community interests and rights too numerous to mention. The organizations involved range from SNCC (Student Non-violent Co-ordinating Committee), CORE (Council on Racial Equality), the Black Panthers, the SCLC (Southern Christian Leadership Council), the

Urban League, the NAACP (National Association for the Advancement of Colored People), to the SDS (Students for a Democratic Society), PAX, Peace and Freedom Party, and include portions (or at times all) of organizations like ADA (Awareness for Democratic Action), UAW (United Auto Workers), and the Welfare Rights movement.

Typically, we cannot say precisely whether this is a movement or a set of related movements. It is a process of social evolution that takes place in the interstices of established organizations; or rather, established organizations become from time to time the instruments through which the movement works itself out.

There is a pattern to the evolution of the movement. Its precursors lie in the radicalism of the 1930s, in the traditional civil rights organizations and in the labor movement. But the new ingredients which began to make themselves felt in the last decade came to their first point of high visibility in the Mississippi summer of 1964, and in the first visible and successful demonstrations and protest marches of Martin Luther King. Here the themes were militant but non-violent activism in the name of civil rights. The events took place in the heart of southern racist country.

The evolution of the movement has proceeded through new pulses of activity centering around new issues. Each new pulse has tended to draw with it new leadership and new groups of participants. The Mississippi summer and the marches and demonstrations in the south gave way to more militant actions in northern ghettos. The Free Speech Movement in Berkeley announced a wave of disruption on university campuses. A small group of college students carried along a more massive following. Civil rights and black power came to be allied with the movement against the war in Vietnam. Clergymen and academics joined blacks and students. Senator McCarthy's candidacy presented a rallying point for the young—but the campaign emphasized the split between the young and the blacks. The withdrawal of President Johnson established the effectiveness of the movement. McCarthy's defeat raised doubts over the validity of 'action within the system'. There was a chain reaction of campus disruptions triggered by SDS, but involving broadening segments of the entire student and faculty populations.

Seen as a system for diffusing innovations, the Movement has had a number of remarkable features:

◆ *It has no clearly established center.* Centers rise and fall on a shifting *ad hoc* basis, around new issues and leaders. At various times, the centers have been Martin Luther King and the SCLC, SNCC, the Free Speech Movement and SDS. In a period of months, centers and leaders emerge, come into prominence, and fade away. Often there appear to be multiple or overlapping centers interacting loosely with one another. A group of college students from Columbia and Cornell undertake an explicit pilgrimage to university campuses to carry a message—the substance and methodology of revolution as they conceive it. But this putative center may be upstaged by the next impetus from an entirely different source.

◆ *Neither is there a stable, centrally established message.* There is no settled content—of theory, technology or methodology—whose diffusion is the movement's work. Instead, there is a shifting and evolving doctrine—a family of related doctrines. Orthodox Marxism, the theory of power elites, the radical sociology of an Alinsky, the radical critique of a man like Naom Chomsky, the doctrines of participation and advocacy, the Black Manifesto, the elaborations of guerilla ideology and tactics, the rationale for mysticism and for the use of drugs, the philosophical radicalism of Marcuse, the essays in radical politics of the New Left, all flow and work together and change rapidly over time. In any given action or event, like the Harvard strike of 1969, it is impossible to separate out clear strands of theory or social innovation whose diffusion is the work of that event. Taking one conceptual threat, for example, the doctrine of racial justice, the history of the message has been manifold and changing, from the militant non-violence of King to the theories of Cleaver and the fragmentation of central doctrine in black nationalism, separatism, black revolution and integrationism. But this shifting and evolving message has proved to be compatible with continuity of action and organization around issues of race.

◆ *The system of the movement cannot be described as the diffusion of an established message from a center to a periphery.* The movement must be seen as a loosely connected, shifting and evolving whole in which centers come and go and messages emerge, rise and fall. Yet the movement transforms both itself and the institutions with which it comes into contact. The movement is a learning system in which both secondary and primary messages evolve rapidly, along with the organization of diffusion itself.

◆ Its remarkable behavior and its international scope depend upon the *infrastructure technology* on the basis of which it operates. It is possible to know at Berkeley tomorrow what happened at Cornell yesterday. Third World factions in Algeria maintain connections with American blacks in Cleveland and in Cuba. Television permits simultaneous international witnessing of events, and makes events 'major' because they are so witnessed. Jet transport permits an international traffic in leaders, spokesmen and participants. An underground press, with readership in the millions, services blacks, students and radicals of all shades and persuasions. Telephones permit connection and coordination of events across the nation. Records, tapes, and transistor radios spread words and music through which all shades of opinion and feeling find expression. Informal networks of students, blacks and radicals employ these technologies to establish a remarkable level of connectedness among individuals, organizations and communities throughout the world. The connectedness permitted by highly developed infrastructure technology allows the movement to retain cohesiveness in the face of shifts in the centers of leadership and the central doctrine. Because of the ease with which innovation can diffuse itself throughout the system as a whole, the movement can adopt an ethos in which transformation around the new is a value in itself.

The learning system of the movement is survival-prone because of its fluidity and its apparent lack of structure. Its ability to transform itself allows it to continue to function with vitality as issues and situations change around it. Its lack of a single fixed center makes it difficult to attack. Its scope is no longer limited by the energy or the resources at the fixed center, nor by the capacity of the 'spokes' connecting the primary center to secondary ones.

Like the constellation firm, the movement represents a set of overlapping and evolving innovations, rather than a set of like instances or applications of a single innovation. Its innovations bear a family resemblance to one another.

Like the business firm organized around a functional system, the movement represents a complex network of components capable of transforming itself by related interacting innovations in its elements. It internalizes what would otherwise be a series of conflicts and interactions among separate systems. In so doing, it raises the potential for systems innovation and raises the level of requirement for critical management and coordination. Both the movement and the business system firm represent network organizations, but what the business system firm accomplishes through formal organization, the movement carries out informally. The business system firm attempts to achieve through formal organization what has grown up in the movement as an informal structure. The movement is to old-style political parties what the business system firm has been to the classical product-based firm of the thirties and forties.

Taking the business systems firm and the movement as family-resembling, though apparently antithetical, models of learning systems, we discover an interesting contrast with classical models for the diffusion of innovation.

Classical models for the diffusion of innovations	_Business systems firms and the movement_
The unit of innovation is a product or technique.	The unit of innovation is a functional system.
The pattern of diffusion is center-periphery.	The pattern of diffusion is systems transformation.
Relatively fixed center and leadership.	Shifting center, _ad hoc_ leadership.
Relatively stable message; pattern of replication of a central message.	Evolving message; family resemblance of messages.
Scope limited by resource and energy at the center and by capacity of 'spokes'.	Scope limited only by infrastructure technology.
'Feedback' loop moves from secondary to primary center and back to all secondary centers.	'Feedback' loops operate locally and universally throughout the systems network.

The principal problem of design shifts from the design of a product or technique to the design of a network. The person's principal allegiance shifts from membership in an organization to membership in a network. And the pattern of social learning shifts from successive 'sweeps' of limited innovations from a center throughout a periphery, to the formation of self-transforming networks.

◆ 5 Government as a learning
◆ system
◆

I Public Learning

The problem of government as a learning system may be stated simply in these terms: how can we, as a society or nation, learn to identify, analyze and solve our problems?

There is more implied here than in the term social learning, as we have so far used it. A social system learns whenever it acquires new capacity for behavior, and learning may take the form of undirected interaction between systems, as in the case of 'the system for keeping us in clean clothes'. But government as a learning system carries with it the idea of *public* learning, a special way of acquiring new capacity for behavior in which government learns for the society as a whole. In public learning, government undertakes a continuing, directed inquiry into the nature, causes and resolutions of our problems.

The need for public learning carries with it the need for a second kind of learning. If government is to learn to solve new public problems, it must also learn to create the systems for doing so and to discard the structure and mechanisms grown up around old problems. The need is not merely to cope with a particular set of new problems, or to discard the organizational vestiges of a particular form of governmental activity which happen at present to be particularly cumbersome. It is to design and bring into being the institutional processes through which new problems can continually be confronted and old structures continually discarded.[1]

Phrased in this way, the problem is government's version of the more general problem of response to the loss of the stable state.

Because many sorts of social system have governments, the requirements of public learning need not be limited to traditional political units. We have already examined what we could now call public learning in the context of the business firm. The concept of public learning applies as well to institutions such as the church, labor unions, schools, hospitals, and social welfare agencies. One way of increasing the capacity for social learning of such decentralized and disconnected social systems has been to equip them with governments—that is, with agencies capable of carrying out directed inquiry for the whole; this is, in fact, a way of describing the movement toward firms organized around business systems.

In our society, however, the most visible and apparently crucial form of public learning *is* carried out by traditional political units, and specifically by the governments of nations. The material of this chapter, whatever its broader implications for public learning, will apply directly to the Federal government of the United States.

Certainly the rhetoric of recent Federal administrations in the United States suggests or directly uses the language of public learning. New administrations enter on platforms made up of lists of public problems that demand solution and policies for solving them. We are forever being exhorted to face up to our problems, to learn from our past, to be wise and persevering in our inquiry, to try new solutions—or we are being reminded that our government is doing these things for us. And this is a use of language that cuts across political parties; it is part of the stock in trade of politics. We even speak of public learning from unexpected events, as in the statement that the United States learned some things from the Great Depression.

There have been over the last decade an increasing

number of signs of concern with our capacity for public learning, for example:

◆ The on-going activity of the task force on reorganization of the Federal Government

◆ Congress's recent study of its own organization

◆ The efforts of the Civil Service Commission to create new categories of Federal employees with ties to the Federal Government rather than to individual agencies

◆ The attempt to introduce broadly across Government the system of program, planning and budgeting first developed in the Department of Defense

◆ During the last two presidential administrations, an acceleration in the rate of creation of new agencies, and of new interagency committees, commissions and planning groups; and within major agencies, a continuing, if fragmented, process of reorganization.

But it is also clear that as a nation we have been dreadfully inept at the process of public learning. This is not particularly attributable to a dearth of ideas for solving our problems. On the contrary, there is a plethora of suggested policies and programs for solving almost any social problem one might care to name. But we have proved ourselves—particularly in the last decade—to be singularly inept at bringing almost any new policy into effect. And we have proved to be equally inept at learning from the mistakes of the past.

The field of housing is a particularly rich mine of evidence for these assertions. Each of the last three presidential administrations has proclaimed its intent to solve the problem of housing supply, particularly for low-income citizens, and under each administration the housing situation has worsened. Moreover, there has been in the last thirty years a series of housing programs (public housing, urban renewal, large-scale rehabilitation) each of which turned away from the perceived failure of the old but was unable to learn from the old how to make its own operations successful.

One could as well have chosen the fields of health services, education, welfare reform, or programs aimed at the elimination of poverty. Each displays an analogous pattern. There is, to be sure, in every case an argument to be made that policies were never adequately tried because resources adequate to them were never made available. But there is also adundant evidence of lack of understanding of the means by which new policies might come into effect. And there is a prevailing attitude toward the recent past which seems to say that failures should be buried and forgotten, or that we should respond to them by a kind of over-learning which consists in veering away from the last in the series.

It is difficult to account for this systematic failure to learn, in view of the acknowledged astuteness of many of the people charged with implementing the new policies and programs. Nor does the explanation lie simply in the familiar 'good people, bad systems'. It seems, rather, to have at least one of its roots in prevailing theory about the implementation of public policy.

If we now draw back to examine the structure of public learning on the part of a specific government, we may regard it from several perspectives. It is at once an informational process, an agent of the implementation and diffusion of policies and programs, a manipulator of policies, and a complex of societies.

As an informational process, the federal government must somehow detect the issues and problems around which it organizes its efforts. It must sense the consequences of what it does. It must organize and transfer within its own system the data and the directives on which policies and programs are based. It must undertake the 'book-keeping' tasks that go with taxation, regulation, and monitoring the state of the systems that are seen to be the legitimate business of government. Moreover, it must maintain this internal and external information system throughout shifts in its environment and in its central problems. These functions fall under what Karl Deutsch has described as the cybernetic model of government.

As an implementer and diffuser of policies, government must formulate and test out policies answering to what it perceives to be the new situations in which it finds itself, and cause these policies to be brought into effect and adapted to the range and scale of situations to which they are relevant.

In manipulating policies, the Federal Government can be seen as an operator of control systems. The 'levers' available to it are within the keyboard of policies derived from acts of Congress and agency practices. These are constantly changing, as Congress passes new laws, amends old, allocates funds, and as officials of the executive branch construct, carry out and modify policies governing administrative practice.

But the Federal Government is also a set of organizations—related to policies and programs as instruments of action; related to one another as organizational neighbors, competitors or collaborators; and related to the people in them as societies in which their working (and much of their non-working) lives are lived.

Each of these ways of looking at the Federal Government reveals a different aspect of the central problem of public learning:

◆   From the point of view of government as an informational system, how do new problems come to attention and ideas about them become ideas in good currency?

◆   From the point of view of government as an agent

of implementation, how are new policies put into action? How are they extended, modified, scaled up? And how are the interconnections between policies understood and controlled as new problems and goals present themselves?

◆ From the point of view of government as a learning system, how are perceptions of the consequences of action fed back into the public learning process?

◆ From the point of view of government as a complex of societies, how are strategies designed and carried out by which resources can be organized to attack new problems, and old structures and mechanisms discarded as obsolete or inhibiting?

The prevailing theory of public learning answers these questions in the following way:

◆ The forming and implementing of public policy is a rational process which takes place in the center-periphery mode.

◆ Issues, once mysteriously established, are taken as given. Inquiry addresses itself to the best policy for tackling an issue, but does not turn back on the relevance and apparent urgency of the issue nor on the processes by which that relevance and urgency came to be perceived.

◆ Similarly, government tends to act as though established policy were stable. Evaluation may address itself to the relative effectiveness or efficiency of the means by which a policy is to be accomplished but seldom (except perhaps on change of administration) to the appropriateness of the policy itself.

◆ The development of a new policy is sharply distinguished from its implementation. In spite of the language of experimentalism, government acts as though the process of invention and adaptation came to an end once a new policy had been legitimized.

◆ Inquiry into new policy, then, is conceived as the primary responsibility of the Federal center. Implementation of policy consists in imposing established policy on a set of peripheral local agencies.

◆ Stable policy exists in compartmentalized units which have their parallels in compartmentalized government agencies. Once new policy has been established, public inquiry tends not to extend across agency boundaries.

◆ The inquiry involved in public learning is conceived in terms of the methods of physical science. Hence, we have the widespread use of scientistic language in which 'problems are defined and quantified', 'hypotheses are developed', 'social experiments are undertaken', 'variables are identified', 'controls established' and 'quantitative measures of outcome formulated'. Finally, 'demonstrations are conducted' and the successful ones are 'replicated'. The answer to the question, 'How shall we undertake public learning?' is increasingly, 'By applying what we take to be scientific method to the formation of public policy.'

Seldom is the prevailing theory made so explicit and seldom is it held in the pure form outlined above. Nevertheless, in one version or another the rational/experimental model of public learning underlies most current thought and practice in the field of public policy, and its inadequacies help to account for our failures in public learning.

It will be our business in this chapter to suggest alternatives to the rational/experimental model,[2] taking as our starting points clues provided by fragments of actual behavior.

II   The emergence of ideas in good currency

Underlying every public debate and every formal conflict over policy there is a barely visible process through
which issues come to awareness and ideas about them
become powerful. The hidden process by which ideas
come into good currency gives us the illusory sense of
knowing what we must worry about and do.

We pay attention to the visible conflicts over policy;
but by the time such a conflict has crystallized, issues
have long since been identified, ideas for solution have
long since been available, sides have been defined and
taken. These antecedent processes are as crucial to the
formation of policy as the processes of discovery in
science are crucial to the formation of plausible hypotheses. But our bias in favor of the rational, the 'scientific', the well-formed and the retrospective causes us to
disregard the less visible process and to accept the ideas
underlying public conflict over policy as mysteriously
given.

The less visible processes, however, are essential to
change in public policy and, in general, to public learning. A learning system must transform its ideas in good
currency at a rate commensurate with its own changing
situation. More broadly, the adequacy of a learning
system is in part shown by how far its ideas in good
currency are adequate to the situation actually confronting it.

It is surprising, in the light of these considerations, how
little curiosity there has been about the emergence of
ideas in good currency.

Some preliminary considerations

Ideas in good currency, as I use the term here, are ideas
powerful for the formation of public policy.[3] Among
their most characteristic features are these: they change
over time; they obey a law of limited numbers; and they

lag behind changing events, sometimes in dramatic ways.

If we take an idea's effectiveness in getting money as a test of its good currency, ideas-in-good-currency in the mid-1950s included 'competition with the Russians', 'the space race', and 'basic research'. By the early 1960s, these had given way to ideas about 'poverty', 'the disadvantaged', and 'unmet public needs'. By the early 1960s, the powerful ideas of the mid-fifties had lost their magic. In order to argue for new policies and to support requests for funds, public entrepreneurs required a new vocabulary and a new set of theories. There was a shift in the language by which people got their money. But there was also a process in which a new set of ideas began to exert its influence; in order to get or keep power, people had to serve these ideas.

The ideas of the early sixties did not simply take their places alongside the ideas of the mid-fifties. The later drove out the earlier, as though ideas in good currency in our society had a limited number of slots. But the process by which this happened was a tortuous one—so much so that at any point along the way we held ideas in good currency inappropriate to our times. City governments in the sixties, for example, failed to bring into good currency ideas adequate to the situation presented by the black center-city. The universities lacked ideas in good currency adequate to the state of mind and behavior of students.

If we take the period of the early sixties and examine ideas in good currency relating to science and technology and the Federal Government, a curious picture emerges. Among the issues taken to be critical in the early sixties and potent, at least in giving rise to Commissions and Committees, were these:

- ◆ The problem of sick industries

- ◆ Automation and its dislocations

+ The scientific and technical manpower shortage
+ The consequences of disarmament.

In 1963 the Kennedy Administration presented to Congress a program known as the Civilian Industrial Technology Program. Its origins and demise I have already described in Chapter 2. The program had grown out of President Kennedy's 14 points for the American textile industry, which had felt itself threatened by imports to the point that it lobbied for higher quotas and tariffs. As a way of extracting certain concessions from the industry, Kennedy offered a program of benefits, among which was Federal support of textile industry research. The CIT program took off from that point.

Over a three year period hostile forces destroyed the CIT program—in a manoeuvre that reveals a great deal about the operation of government-industry systems—but in that same period, the textile industry underwent a change. Overall demand for textiles increased, partly due to the increasing requirements of the Vietnam war and partly because of an overall increase in demand stemming from economic prosperity. It was a common joke in the industry that the textile business was like sex: when it was good, it was marvelous; and when it was bad, it was very nice. The concept of the textile industry as a 'sick industry' disappeared from the scene and with it the public sense of need for Federal research support.

In the early 1960s, the Automation Commission came into being, out of the merging of a series of concerns drawn from Congressional committees and expressed in a variety of Bills. Its title—the Commission on Automation, Economic Progress and Technological Change—reflects some of this diversity of origin. The Commission was formed on the Noah's Ark principal—two negroes, two labor leaders, two industrialists, two women, and the like—and began its deliberations at a time when the national unemployment rate stood at approximately 6 per cent. It began in a climate of deep concern about automation (sometimes used by Commission members as a synonym for technological change) and the dislocations caused by it.

During the life of the Commission, two parallel streams of events occurred. The Bureau of Labor Statistics investigated the rate of change of productivity in the United States over about the last 20 years, and revealed that (by its calculations) the rate remained roughly constant at 2·5 per cent. During the same period of time, the unemployment rate dropped from approximately 6 per cent to approximately 4 per cent.

The burning issue of automation seemed to have evaporated. The Commission produced many volumes of analysis and a wide range of recommendations—including the more recently celebrated recommendation for a national effort towards social indicators (that is, toward the development of measures of social performance, comparable to 'Gross National Product' as a measure of economic performance)—but it did not recommend a major national remedy for the dislocations of automation.

In the late 1950s, it was not uncommon in scientific and engineering circles to hear talk of the impending shortage of scientific and technical manpower. The research and development budget had been growing (at a rate which, wags said, would cause it to intersect with the GNP by 1970); defense research and development had made enormous demands on the nation's technical manpower supply; critics were already concerned about the needs of university research; and it was feared now that NASA's growing needs would exhaust the nation's remaining supply of scientists and engineers, leaving other significant national requirements unmet.

Under the leadership of Dr James Killian, a Committee on Scientific and Technical Manpower came into being, under the aegis of the National Academy of

Sciences. During the life of this committee, however, several concurrent events occurred: minor cutbacks (or rather, decreases in the rate of growth) took place in defense spending, releasing some hundreds (or perhaps thousands—the numbers were never entirely clear) of engineers claimed to be walking the streets of Los Angeles and Long Island. And students—apparently under the influence of sustained public discussion of growing demands for scientists and engineers—were alleged to be shifting toward increased enrollment in graduate schools of science and engineering.

The shortage of scientific and technical manpower did not so much disappear as dissolve. When the report of the Committee was published in the mid-sixties, its qualified conclusions did not give rise to further Federal action.

On the other hand, the problem of alleged cutbacks in defense spending—with their feared consequences for defense-based industry—became the subject of deliberation for a new inter-agency committee, whose conclussions, in turn, faded from view as the Vietnam conflict developed.

Ideas in good currency emerge *in time*, and the situations to which they refer change underneath the very process of deliberation. Not infrequently, the changes take place as a result of public debate and attention.

Ideas are often slow to come into good currency; and, once in good currency and institutionalized, they are slow to fade away. By the time ideas have come into good currency, they often no longer accurately reflect the state of affairs.

One of the principal criteria for effective learning systems is precisely the ability of a social system to reduce this lag so that ideas in good currency reflect present problems.[4] It becomes all the more imperative, therefore, to gain an understanding of the ways in which this semi-visible process works.

Themes of the process

I will not attempt here either a full-fledged theory or a complete case history. There are, however, some fairly general themes of the process which, taken together, provide a projective model against which particular instances can be compared.

The essence of the model is this:

Taken at any given time, a social system is dynamically conservative in its structural, technological and conceptual dimensions. This last represents the 'system' of ideas in good currency. Characteristically, what precipitates a change in that system of powerful ideas is a disruptive event or sequence of events, which sets up a demand for new ideas in good currency. At that point, ideas already present in free or marginal areas of the society begin to surface in the mainstream, mediated by certain crucial roles. The broad diffusion of these new ideas depends upon interpersonal networks and upon media of communication, all of which exert their influence on the ideas themselves. The ideas become powerful as centers of policy debate and political conflict. They gain widespread acceptance through the efforts of those who push or ride them through the fields of force created by the interplay of interests and commitments. Inquiry now becomes a political process in which the movement of ideas to power goes hand in hand with bids for dominance. When the ideas are taken up by people already powerful in society this gives them a kind of legitimacy and completes their power to change public policy. After this, the ideas become an integral part of the conceptual dimension of the social system and appear, in retrospect, obvious.

Crisis There is, to begin with, some critical shift in situation which threatens the social system and sets up a demand for new ideas which will explain, diagnose or remedy the crisis. The analogy with scientific inquiry is helpful. The 'crisis' here is a piece of disruptive evidence incompatible with accepted theory which for some reason cannot be ignored. The Michelson-Morley experiment concerning the speed of light was a famous case in point, as was Galileo's observation of the mountains of the moon, Ticho Brahe's observations of the orbits of the planets, the recent discoveries of multiple subatomic particles, in Darwin's time the geological data concerning the age of the earth. Each of these confronted the scientific community with the failure of accepted theory and raised the potential for new ideas in good currency.[5]

There is a social system of science, underlying its visible theoretical dimension, and there is conversely a theoretical dimension to every social system which contains the social system's view of itself, its role and function within some larger system, the nature of its environment, its own operation, and the norms which govern its behavior. As in the case of scientific theory, then, a 'crisis' for the social system is any happening perceived to be incompatible with this prevailing theory.[6]

But, as we have seen, dynamically conservative systems normally protect themselves against ideas which cannot be brought to public attention without disruptive consequences. Think, for example, of the history of the concepts of psychoanalysis or of the welfare state, or indeed of any set of ideas perceived as threatening prevailing institutions. The means of protection vary. Ideas may be relegated to private spheres or to the margins of society. Where ideas have not yet penetrated the general consciousness but suggest themselves on all sides, they may be repressed—that is, held back from conscious attention —or, like ideas discussed under headings such as philosophy or change, they may be relegated to a kind of intellectual never-never land, disconnected from action. Where ideas have become subjects of explicit attention, at least on the part of a few, those people may be suppressed, forcibly prevented from entering the arenas of public inquiry and debate. The movement from repression to suppression[7] is a characteristic pattern in the emergence of ideas in good currency; as the ideas become more powerful, the defense against them shifts.

Events come to function as crises in the sense used here only when forces working toward the perception of them somehow overcome these protective mechanisms. For American society at large, the war in Vietnam is such an event, as is the revolutionary behavior of a large part of American youth. These events disrupt not only by rocking the boat of civil order but by jarring settled ways of looking at society.

Such a disruption does not immediately overturn established theory. There is usually a substantial lag between perception of the disruptive phenomena and reorganization of prevailing theory. The lag may be counted in months, years (as in the case of the ideas relating to policy for science and technology) or decades. Gradually, efforts to ignore or repress the crisis give way to a realization of its existence, its incompatibility with settled ways of looking at things, and its danger to the social system. At this stage, there is widespread readiness for new ideas.

Attention turns then to certain free areas within the social system. These are backwaters in which ideas have been able to germinate without encountering massive defenses. They are the margins of society. Freud, for example, during the time he was working on *The Interpretation of Dreams* existed, in the medical and the larger social worlds of Vienna, as a marginal man. Norman Thomas occupied a marginal position in American life for decades until his ideas (not his person) found their way into the mainstreams of public policy.

The social system tolerates, to a greater or lesser extent, in marginal areas or in playful or innocuous form, or in relatively insulated groups, ideas which would be virulent and disruptive if released into the main arteries

of the culture. Then, crises in the system permit or com-
pel these ideas to come to public notice and to begin
their progress toward public awareness, currency, and
acceptance. Ideas about mystical experience, communes
and enhancement of experience through drugs survived
in the United States for generations in small sects only
to be taken up in a massive and public way in the sixties.
In the forties and fifties, radical critiques of America's
poverty, decaying cities, and neglected needs in the
public sector, survived in a submerged and compartmentalized way to emerge in the sixties as broad-based
critique and (in the Kerner Commission Report) as
public gospel. Throughout America's sexually conservative years, liberal attitudes towards the human body survived in relatively invisible enclaves because most people
were able to regard their adherents as cranks. In the
sixties these attitudes emerged as a powerful threat to
established morality.[8]

Vanguard roles   The movement of ideas from free areas
to the mainstream has nothing automatic about it.
Ideas do behave as if they had a life of their own, but
only through the efforts of those who use and are used
by ideas. Vanguards move ideas to public awareness,
supplying the energy necessary to raise them over the
threshold of public consciousness. But within and among
these vanguards, there is a multiplicity of roles.

The muckraker forces us to look at the disruptive instance, takes it out of the domain of private experience
and thrusts it into broad public view as Michael Har-
rington did for poverty in America, Robert Coles for
hunger and desolation in the Mississippi Delta, and
Ralph Nader for the abuses of the manufacturers of
consumer products. The muckraker is like the scientist
who forces the scientific community to pay attention to
a piece of evidence incompatible with prevailing theory.

The artist gives us new ways of looking at our experience, new ways of defining ourselves in relation to reality,

and in the process frees our awareness of phenomena incompatible with settled theory. In Marshall Mc-
Luhan's language, he shifts our gaze from the 'rear view
mirror' to experience of the here-and-now, as Cubism
gave us a vision of things in the image of the new industrial forms, or as James Joyce helped us to become atten-
tive to things in our own experience that depth psycholo-
gists were at roughly the same time beginning to explain.

The utopian presents us with a vision of what might
be, in such a way as to focus attention on the inadequacy
of what is—either directly, by contrasting a better future
with an inadequate present, or ironically, by presenting
as future a concentrated picture of present evils. Bellamy
in *Looking Backward* and Skinner in *Walden II* were primarily in the first mode, while Orwell in *1984* and Von-
negut in *Player Piano* were primarily in the second.

The prophet—whether in his Old Testament form or
in the current ecological style—tells us where we are
going, makes us treat as real and present the distant consequences of our current behavior, and through appeal
to morality confronts us with sins we would otherwise
have ignored or repressed.

The vanguard roles need not be mutually exclusive, of
course. Samuel Butler was both prophet and utopian.
But the nature of the vanguard roles and the crises to
which they call attention vary with the type of idea in
good currency.

The idea may be a way of looking at a particular
situation, one that has implications for public action: for
example, the pricing policies of the drug industry, the
condition of mental hospitals, hunger and malnutrition
in rural America. Then the crisis is a particular event,
practice or institution incompatible with prevailing
theory, and the muckraker's role is primary.

Or the idea may be in the nature of an invention. In
this case, the *idea* of the invention undergoes a process of
coming to awareness, diffusion, debate and acceptance

which is at once distinct from and interdependent with the innovation and diffusion of the invention itself. The crisis may be a particular inequity to which the invention is a response; the scandalous condition of mental hospitals, for example, led to the invention of community mental health centers. Or it may be a disruption of some functional system; automobiles changed patterns of settlement and access to the center city, and the suburban shopping center has been a responsive invention. The important vanguard role here is a kind of prophet; Buckminster Fuller, with his 'Dymaxicon' car and house, has been a prophet of technological change.

The idea may be in the nature of intermediate theory, theory that serves as a bridge connecting views of particular situations to what we will later call paradigms of change. The bridging function of intermediate theory is essential to public learning. For those who operate under a revolutionary paradigm in a particular community, there must be a theory of the community that connects it to the paradigm. If the paradigm requires 'establishment', 'disadvantaged', and 'community leadership', then an interpretive process must identify these elements within the community. Otherwise the paradigm cannot engage the community situation. A man like Saul Alinsky plays in communities like Chicago's Woodlawn district the role of formulator and purveyor of such an intermediate theory, whose function is to connect Woodlawn to the paradigm of revolution. He is at once muckraker and utopian, and the crisis to which he responds has its roots in the discrepancy between the reality of communities like Woodlawn and the prevailing norms of equity in our society. Without such a connection the paradigms have no potency, no matter how strongly they are held.[9]

Within the theoretical dimension of a social system, ideas operate at different levels. At the most fundamental level, every social system has root concepts which underlie all theory-making. These are in the nature of metaphors like mechanism, technique and progress which in the last several hundred years have cut across most sectors and subcultures of society. As new root concepts move into good currency their influence on the larger social system is enormous, since they influence not only a particular public policy, practice or situation, but the entire range of activities and practices of the system as a whole. These root concepts are like the largest overriding waves of change. They overshadow the smaller perturbations due to innovations related to particular institutions, inventions, or pieces of intermediate theory. The vanguard roles associated with root concepts are those of artist, scientist, philosopher, whose contribution is to make us alter our most fundamental views of things; and the crises to which they respond are the disequilibria associated with the deepest patterns of structural, theoretical and technological change.

Where 'idea' may have four such disparate meanings, not only the nature of the vanguard roles and related crises but the time-scales for emergence in good currency must vary enormously. Alinsky's ideas about Woodlawn began to penetrate Woodlawn itself in less than a year. Ralph Nader's views of the abuses of the automotive industry came to public awareness in about five years. Buckminster Fuller's technological prophecies took over twenty years to reach national attention. The time required for the development of widespread awareness of the cluster of theories associated with mechanism or progress must be numbered in half-centuries.

Diffusion of ideas   The creation of widespread public awareness demands the diffusion of ideas, a process distinct both from the process by which ideas become powerful and from the diffusion of the practices to which ideas relate. At the time of this writing, for example, the ideas of certain inventions—the electric car, the environmentally controlled city, the programmed transportation system—begin to diffuse broadly throughout society, well in advance of their becoming powerful for public policy and well in advance of the widespread adoption of the inventions themselves.

In this process, media are central. They are the vehicles of the vanguard roles, the technologies of diffusion. They have their own thresholds and place their own criteria on the formulation of ideas to be diffused. These requirements are not merely technical. There are journalistic requirements that events fit the prevailing myths of news. There are semantic requirements for 'catchiness'. The very ability to express an idea in a phrase—Medicare, the War on Poverty, Guaranteed Annual Wage—may be critical. Through such requirements, media transform the ideas themselves.

The brokers of ideas, equally important to diffusion, adapt and translate ideas as they pass them along from one sub-system to another or from a sub-culture to the larger society. They are consultants, popularizers, interpreters, critics and analysts whose brokerage channels are the informal networks that connect segments of society to one another.

In general, the pattern of diffusion is neither straightforward nor homogeneous. Ideas are waves that engulf broad areas of society, but they do so unevenly depending on the susceptibility of subcultures to *that* idea (Women's Liberation, the Ecological Crisis, Guaranteed Income) and on the varying permeability of subcultures to new ideas in general. This difference in permeability to new ideas defines subcultural boundaries and, again, exerts its influence on the ideas themselves.

Struggle for acceptance When an idea gains public attention, it does not thereby become potent for change in policy. Its power is manifest when it is not only broadly recognized and publicized but when it has become an issue for debate, when organizations begin to grow around it, and when it begins to be used to gain influence and money.

Ideas—concerning, for example, the legalization of marijuana or abortion—may become powerful for public policy long before they gain broad acceptance. And ideas may gain power as well as attention for one group before another. The differences in the relative potency of ideas such as 'establishment', 'elite', 'progress', 'success', 'social justice', 'equity', 'minorities', 'racism' and the like, go a long way toward defining the oppositions in our society between black and white, young and old, radical and liberal. What we find to be ideas in good currency, then, depends on whether we examine family, friendship groups, organizations, neighborhoods, broad subcultures (like 'black culture' or 'youth culture'), the nation as a whole or the vast and nebulous entity called 'world opinion'.

If ideas are to become powerful for change in policy, they must enter a field of competing forces. To the extent that ideas enter channels leading to public consideration in such a way as to threaten a social system, they stir up conflict, formal or informal. At this stage in the emergence of ideas in good currency, there is a central place for the roles of champion and defender.

The short but instructive career of the 'COMSAT' for Housing illustrates something of these roles and their interactions.

During President Johnson's administration the Department of Housing and Urban Development (HUD) held a summer conference on Science and the City. Out of this conference came a design for a national quasi-public institution, modeled on the Communications Satellite Corporation, to tackle massive low-income housing goals.

COMSAT for Housing had a champion, Hortense Gabel, who, in order to develop the idea, assembled a team of architects, planners, systems analysts, and housers. She pressed for the idea's acceptance, formally and informally, through successively higher levels of HUD.

She succeeded in organizing presentations and reviews for the Undersecretary and Secretary. Not surprisingly, she produced mixed results. Partisans and opponents of the idea emerged within the hierarchy. Partisans battled to overcome internal opposition and bring the idea to the attention of the White House staff and finally to the President.

Opponents argued over the idea's workability, its impact on the housing industry, its centralization of power. But underneath the surface of the argument, attack and defense reflected personal enmities and alliances and concerns about dominance or devotion. The idea engaged HUD. It split the organization into parties according to intellectual and ideological positions, political and personal interests. In this context, the champion presented the idea in its most favorable light, talked to each advocate or defender in the terms of his greatest interest, built alliances, made judgments about the timing of confrontations.

Thanks to these manoeuvres, the idea made its way to the White House and seemed about to gain acceptance as administration policy until a leak to the *New York Times* caused President Johnson to withdraw his support. The idea continued to exert its influence, however. Elements of it have found their way into other housing proposals and into some ongoing programs.

The story of the COMSAT for Housing has parallels in thousands of comparable efforts to introduce new ideas into situations where they will effect change in public policy. It is comparable in some ways to the history of the Civilian Industrial Technology Program or to the Automation Commission. As creation of awareness and diffusion of concept give way to the effort to gain acceptance, a new sort of game begins to be played. Attack and defense, championship and resistance, become the dominant modes. The fields of force within institutions condition the moves and their outcomes. Failure to win the

game in a particular institutional battle does not, of
course, condemn an idea to permanent rejection. Ideas
lend themselves to repeated battles as changed political
situations offer new opportunities. And even when an
idea dies in a particular form, it may continue to influence succeeding ideas, as the idea of the COMSAT itself
influenced the formation of the COMSAT for Housing.

The three previous sections support the distinction between the processes by which ideas come to awareness,
diffuse and gain power. But these processes also inter-
relate. The diffusion of an idea like COMSAT made it
easier for a COMSAT for Housing to surface in HUD.
That idea spread as it became a center of controversy and
gained acceptance. In fact, the two processes fed on each
other; diffusion led to conflict and conflict nourished
diffusion.

Invasions Given this warlike process, it is not surprising that ideas in good currency change as one social
system invades another. In combat with the dynamically
conservative system, the invader replaces the internal
champion. Ideas (or systems of ideas) move, through in-
vaders, into the invaded culture, transforming as they go.

As they cross cultural boundaries they take on the
character of metaphor. As lawyers in the last decade became increasingly involved in representation of the poor,
'advocacy' found its way into 'advocacy planning',
'medical advocacy', and the like. Legal advocacy became a projective model for new kinds of relationships
between citizens and professionals. The concept of 'ombudsman' travelled a similar path. The biological concept of ecology invades planning and urban studies. In
each case the idea transforms itself as it shifts from one
field to another. The 'ecology of the city' is not an
ecology in the biological sense, and 'advocacy planning'
is in many ways unlike legal advocacy. But the idea from
the donor culture serves in the recipient culture as a

nucleus for the evolution of a new idea in good currency.

Politics of inquiry Whether it occurs through internal championships or invasion or both, the struggle of ideas in good currency to gain acceptance has not only an intellectual but a political dimension. In order to gain acceptance ideas must tap into sources of power. They are also vehicles through which persons and agencies gain power. When individuals push or ride ideas they also seek to establish their own dominance.

It is interesting to consider the process through which a small group moves as it tackles and begins to resolve a relatively unstructured problem. Leadership, if it is there, shows itself in the way ideas move into good currency, in the championship or defense of ideas, in nurturing the process of problem-solving. If leadership is indeterminate, it may develop through the problem-solving process itself. Characteristically, ideas, perspectives and solutions compete, and in the same process ideas and persons emerge as dominant. It is as though the struggle for authority were a facet of the problem-solving process. There is here, perhaps, the seed of an explanation of the law of limited numbers.

Within a social system at a given time there are never very many ideas in good currency, just as there are never very many fashions. It is as though a social system had for ideas in good currency a limited number of slots. This law of limited numbers clearly has one basis in our limited ability to absorb and tolerate ideas. It has another in the fact that potent ideas make incompatible demands on time, energy, and resources. But there are, in addition, limits to the 'role slots' for leadership. If ideas come into good currency through a process in which some people come to dominate others, we can understand why there is at any given time in a social system a limited number of slots for powerful ideas and why powerful new ideas drive old ones out.

Legitimization Ideas need finally to be legitimized if they are to become embodied in public policy. If ideas are to gain entry to the limited set of channels through which formal policy changes flow, they require, in the approval of administrators, commissions, notable personages, legislators and the like, a kind of benediction. The benediction is essential and it is seldom automatic. Those who can confer it use their authority as scarcely as Congress uses its power of the purse. The decision to grant it springs ordinarily from a shared calculation of the idea's relation to personal and political interests and of the power it has already amassed. The refusal to grant it may kill an idea, at least for a time and in a particular form, as in the case of the COMSAT for Housing. The decision to grant it later may produce, as in the case of the 'technical manpower shortage', the absurd effect of a newly legitimized idea clearly out of step with its times.

Systems of ideas Ideas often travel not alone, but in pairs, clusters or systems. Often it is difficult to determine where one idea leaves off and another begins, and therefore to apply the law of limited numbers.

In recent American experience, for example, the notion of community control is a theme with many variations, not all mutually compatible. The movement to community control turns out to be composed of many sub-movements differing in goals, strategy, and style.

At any given time, ideas in good currency may form a system, a set of compatible and mutually reinforcing ideas related to one another as interlocking aspects of a single policy. More likely, a set of differentiated notions —like 'community-based health center', 'children's center,' 'headstart,' 'neighborhood health center'—represent variants of a single theme—decentralization of services—which, at a quite general level, is in the air. Ideas like 'advocacy', 'ombudsmen', 'COMSAT', may pop up in agency after agency or in segment after segment of policy not through a concerted effort at diffusion, but through independent efforts to latch on to an idea of emerging potency. Such as idea may seem to burst full-blown on the scene, as 'ombudsman' did in the mid-sixties, or it may emerge through a kind of mimesis out of a variety of generalizations from specific situations, projects, demonstrations, presentations, experiments and the like.

Whether ideas in good currency take the form of a system, or of a theme and variations, they unquestionably reveal, at any given time, a family resemblance which testifies to the overlapping and mutually interactive processes by which they came to be.

At bottom, this family resemblance may stem from the environmental, technological, economic and class-related conditions of the society. We cannot separate the theoretical dimension of a social system from its structure and culture.

The purpose of this analysis, however, has been to suggest that the emergence of ideas in good currency, as a process, has certain characteristic features, regardless of the content of the ideas in question and regardless of the conditions from which they spring.

Responses to the pathologies of ideas in good currency It is tempting to argue that reform of the process through which ideas come into good currency must consist in elimination of the non-rational factors—that is, of anything that detracts from simple awareness of the troublesome features of situations confronting the social system. But this is neither possible nor desirable.

For one thing, the issues taken to be important at any given time represent a selection from a total body of information which is of enormous complexity. The inventory of issues in good currency is never adequate to the situation; it never succeeds in exhausting what might be the set of issues to be drawn from that situation. The ultimate basis of this fact is epistemological; there is simply more in the situation than can be conceptually

abstracted from it. Because one never comes to the end
of listing the issues inherent in the situation, there must
be some basis for selection. The selection cannot be made
on the criteria of 'what is most important', because this
would imply a complete inventory of available issues,
from which the most important were to be selected; and
such a complete inventory is not feasible. Issues can indeed be selected as important, on some criteria, but there
is a level of arbitrariness here, because other issues,
equally important, might also be selected. The political
meaning of issues—their relation to the effort to gain or
keep power—aids in the process of selection. The politics
of inquiry is endemic to the emergence of ideas in good
currency.

But there are pathologies of the process that lead to
inertial life and to premature abandonment of issues.
These are protected by the scientific mythology under
which we treat the issues as given, and cut off from
inquiry the process leading to their emergence. The
given-ness of ideas in good currency is, in effect, a variant of the myth of the stable state.

There is also our need for a façade of progress and
problem-solving. Government seems to need to operate
always under an aura of rational, active work on what
are taken to be public problems; and, moreover, to be
perceived as making progress in that work. This has the
effect of inducing premature abandonment of issues. If
we are not solving them, we must at least give the
appearance of progress by moving on to the next batch.
It tends to be true of government, as of philosophy, that
old questions are not answered—they only go out of
fashion.

Often these myths are coupled with the further myth of
'once-and-for-all' solutions—the belief that we can come
to the end of the problems to be dealt with. Hence, the
language, for example, of 'elimination of poverty', when
it is quite clear that poverty is a relative condition which

behaves on a kind of Maslow-scale, needs fulfilled simply leading to the clear and present perception of further needs requiring, with equal urgency, to be met.

And there are certain related pathologies of the process which tend to keep government from knowing what is happening, even when it has no clear political interest in avoiding this knowledge. In their resultant effect, these myths and pathologies lock government into issues that have been identified, or they induce it to move on to the next issue while the old ones remain equally urgent and unresolved. Although the politics of inquiry cannot be dispensed with, its pathologies are intolerable in an era of loss of the stable state.

While the remedies are unclear, we can identify some directions in which to reach for them:

◆ *Increased public attention to the process by which ideas come into good currency* The pathologies described above depend upon the obscurity of this process both to the general public and to much of government. Reform requires, first, recognition that there is such a process and that it is susceptible to certain kinds of influence. The nature of that influence may itself become a political issue of importance.

◆ *Support of the vanguard roles, of marginality, of brokers of ideas* Given our analysis of the process by which ideas come into good currency, any concern over helping the process must address itself to key actors within it. And these key actors tend to occupy roles in the free areas of society, to be marginal in relation to established systems, or to occupy the vanguard roles of prophet, muckraker, artist and critic. It may be futile to call for increased support by established interests who find themselves threatened by the very roles in question. But there is enough difference of perceived interest on the part of many of the institutions capable of such support to permit increase in the overall level of support.

◆ *Reform of the design and implementation of the process of evaluation* as it affects determination of the relevance of issues and of policies designed to deal with them.

◆ *Modification of elements of the social system of government* in order to counter forces which support the inertial life of ideas in good currency.

The last two points will be discussed in later sections of this chapter.

III   Implementation of policy

Ideas powerful for action may lead to the formation of a policy and then to its broad application. The problem of carrying out a policy is in many ways a version of the diffusion of innovation, a version in which the innovation is a new policy and the agent of diffusion is a government. It is not surprising, then, that in the dominant, center-periphery model of policy implementation, 'central' first defines a policy and then takes responsibility for spreading it.

The center-periphery model of the implementation of policy may take a variety of forms, depending on the level of specificity at which the new policy is initially defined, the role of central, and the ways in which behavior at the periphery is sanctioned and monitored.

1 *Promulgate a policy*   Here, central simply sets forth the policy it desires—for example, the restriction of business investments abroad, or the involvement of business in ghetto problems. There is no invoking of sanctions, no monitoring for compliance, and no provision of resources from a central agency. It is assumed that the simple exhortation to behave in a certain way will elicit the desired behavior.

price Controls

2 *Seed demonstrations* Central creates first instances of the desired behavior and assumes that others at the periphery will imitate them until the new policy has spread adequately over the territory.

3 *Provide teachers* Central defines the new policy and then provides teachers, trainers or consultants to assist local agents in carrying it out.

4 *Provide resources* Central defines the new policy and provides the resources it believes necessary for implementation. These may take the form of money, or more specific forms such as contraceptives for birth control or fertilizer for farming. The new policy may be defined at a high level of specificity and the resources given directly to implementing agents. Or the new policy may be defined only in very broad terms and the resources given to intermediate agents for their further distribution; in this case the model approximates to block grants and revenue sharing. In both cases, it is assumed that local agents know how to carry out the policy, or can learn; that they will want to carry out the policy without compulsion; and that they are prevented from carrying it out by the absence of resources which they cannot be expected to get for themselves.

In each of these models, central avoids sanctions or monitoring and takes only those initiatives required for local agents to learn the new behavior. Each model represents a different view of the required initiative.

5 *Enforce the law* Here it is assumed that local agents will know how to do what is desired and will not want to do it. Policies are promulgated in the form of laws and systems established to monitor and enforce compliance. The policy may prohibit certain kinds of behavior (drunkenness, for example) or it may command positive behavior (maintenance of property to standard). Punishments may vary from imprisonment to the withdrawal of funds. In each instance, it is assumed that central need provide no resources or teachers, and that the threat of

punishment will be enough to induce and sustain the desired behavior.

6 *Extend central control into the periphery*   Action cannot be left to local agents, regardless of the nature of the sanctions or the supports provided. In order to produce the desired behavior, central must incorporate the local agents into its own organization. Central's relation to local agent now becomes that of central to regional office or of grantor to grantee. Resources, teaching support and sanctions may flow from central to the local agents, but always within the framework of central's administrative control.

The six center-periphery models of policy implementation are types, amenable to many different combinations. Teachers and resources may be provided together, for example, or combined with demonstrations or with punishment for non-compliance. Different models may be applied to the several phases of policy implementation. One model may be used to generate plans, for example, another to produce first instances of action and yet another to maintain long-term behavior. The use of particular models or combinations will reflect judgments about key assumptions—whether new behavior can be elicited from local agents, independent of central; the extent to which central must keep local agencies under continuing control; the disposition of local agencies to behave according to the new policy; the means by which a central agency can induce or control behavior in many local agencies; the resources available and needed to carry out the policy; the stance central takes in relation to local agents; and the nature of existing systems in the localities for implementing policy.

All of the center-periphery models and their combinations share, to a greater or lesser extent, the assumptions that policy exists fully defined prior to its implementation; that policy is to be applied uniformly in all localities, at least in broad outline; and that management of the process of implementation belongs, in critical ways, to central. All of the models rest on theories of learning; they depend on certain beliefs about the ways in which central can induce local agents to behave in conformity to policy. Each model lends itself to distortion in practice just to the extent that its assumptions and theories do not hold.

Propose-dispose

There is a particular version of the center-periphery model, broadly and powerfully held at least in the United States, in which central formulates specifications for a new policy, makes funds available for its implementation, and solicits proposals from local agents for behavior conforming to the policy. Central then rewards certain proposers with funding, punishes others by withholding funds, and proceeds to monitor the behavior of local agents for conformity to proposal. Withdrawal of continued funding is the sanction invoked to enforce compliance. There is sometimes the further notion that the local agents will, after a time, secure their own resources to continue implementing the policy.

The attraction of the propose-dispose variant lies in its intermediate position between tightly coupled and loose, non-controlling relationships between center and periphery. The model recognizes that central cannot or should not assume the role of local agent, and that compulsion alone will not be sufficient to induce the desired behavior. It solicits the desired behavior, therefore, but introduces an element of compulsion through the carrots and sticks represented by the granting or withholding of funds. The model also represents an approach to the generation of new policy. Where central can specify the broad outlines of the desired behavior but cannot describe it in detail, it may ask local agents to fill in the blanks.[10]

In the propose-dispose model, central does assume

that many local agents can be stimulated to behave in accordance with central policy through the promise of reward and the threat of punishment. In this sense, the model rests on a behavioral theory of learning which has been associated with the names of Pavlov, Watson and Skinner: the trainer first elicits behavior by setting up a situation in which the subject is moved, by fear of punishment or hope of reward, to improvise; the desired behavior is then selected and progressively stamped in by continuing reward, while punishment eliminates undesirable behavior. When it is applied to the broad implementation of policy, the propose-dispose model raises the special problem of a government 'trainer' who must somehow train at a distance a large number of dispersed subjects. It is as though Skinner were to train a thousand pigeons widely dispersed throughout the country.

At each step of the process, the propose-dispose model depends for its effectiveness on certain additional assumptions:

- ◆ It is feasible for central to generate broad new policy which will be applicable to many dispersed localities.

- ◆ It is possible to stimulate an adequate number of conforming proposals by disseminating central specifications coupled with the promise of monetary reward.

- ◆ It is feasible and economic to control widely dispersed local behavior by some form of monitoring and enforcement.

- ◆ Local behavior will continue to conform to the proposal after the monitoring period is over.

We can explore the validity of these assumptions, as well as the more fundamental set of assumptions which go to make up the rational center-periphery theory of policy implementation, in the context of a particular Federal program.

The State Technical Services Act

In 1965, Congress enacted a bill called the State Technical Services Act, whose stated purpose was to increase industrial productivity by disseminating advanced technology throughout American industry. The Act recognized that large industry tended to be more effective in its use of new technology than small industry, defense-related industry more effective than civilian industry, and industry close to the big cities more effective than industry in less populous areas. The Act aspired to equity in the use of new technology. It sought to cause new technology to flow into industries and geographical areas relatively poor in technology.

The Act assumed that a kind of technological vacuum existed in certain companies, industries and regions, and set out to fill this vacuum by forging bonds between industry and the universities.

In this respect, the Act was a version of a very old idea. The first Morrill Act, which launched the Agricultural Extension program, also included an Industrial one. It called for the establishment of industrial experimental stations, industrial extension programs in the Land Grant Colleges, and industrial extension agents, all parallel to the agricultural extension model. But the industrial side of the Morrill Act remained substantially unrealized. In the hundred years between the Morrill Act and the mid-1960s, union proponents unsuccessfully advanced about twenty different versions of the industrial extension program.

The generation of the State Technical Services Act was itself a complex process which lasted well over two years.

At the time of the drafting of the Act, there were about fourteen local programs in State and Land Grant

institutions which served as prototypes for what might be
done under State Technical Services. Their activities included consultancy, technical assistance, trouble shoot-
ing, short courses, and the dissemination of information;
and their clients tended to be small firms located in relatively non-industrial States, such as Georgia, North Carolina and Missouri. They supported the new bill.

But there were many other actors involved in the process that led eventually to the bill's passage:

- The powerful Land Grant College Association. It
  wanted to capture the program in order to build
  up established departments of university extension.

- The agricultural colleges and the agricultural extension agents associated with them (some 70,000
  of them still in the field in 1965). Agricultural extension, feeling many of its traditional functions
  slipping away, saw in the program an opportunity
  to diversify into growing sectors of the economy.

- University libraries and technical librarians and
  the multiple associations to which they belonged.
  These saw in the program an opportunity to build
  libraries and instal new methods of processing information: they saw the process of technological
  innovation and diffusion as a problem in informa-
  tion-dissemination.

- Industrial development agencies in the various
  States, and their associations, who saw industrial
  development as a matter of attracting industry to
  new State locations.

- Some State Governors, particularly those from
  rural States, saw the program as a politically attractive contribution to economic development,
  were anxious to receive their share, and felt strongly the need to counterbalance the trends of move-

ment of investment and industry toward the large centers of population.

♦ Within the Federal Government itself, there were interactions with the Department of Agriculture, the Council of Economic Advisors, the Economic Development Agency, the Small Business Administration, the Bureau of the Budget, and the office of the President's Science Advisor. The last two played the role of mediator of the conflicts engendered by the program.

♦ Business organizations, such as the Chamber of Commerce, and national professional and engineering organizations, who saw in the program a potential threat to free enterprise and to the hegemony of large corporations, or who felt it was simply another Federal boondoggle.

The effort to get the legislation passed was very much a process of manoeuvring among these actors, whose interests conflicted and overlapped. In the process, the Act was shaped in a way that gave a high degree of control to existing State organizations, such as State Universities and Land Grant Colleges, and made for an equitable distribution of monies among the States, with a preferential attitude toward the less populous and industrialized. These elements reflected the need to please senators from the rural States. In addition, the program veered away from anything that looked like product development or technological innovation; this was to counter opposition from private industry. The Act leaned heavily in the direction of teaching, technical assistance and the dissemination of information.

In the months immediately following the passage of the bill, the Department of Commerce solicited proposals for projects which were to be pilots for the broader program. Universities, colleges and independent non-profit institutions submitted proposals, of which only a limited number could be funded. The great bulk of proposals were from university departments of extension and from university libraries. These proposed, for the most part, to continue what they had already been doing, even though their short courses and dissemination of documents were precisely what had *not* made significant contributions to the industrial use of advanced technology. Many of these proposals were rejected with the comment that they were not sufficiently innovative in their approach to the problem. Back came proposals with a veneer of innovative rhetoric, covering essentially similar content.

An advisory committee had been formed, incorporating representatives of many of those institutions that had supported the bill. Representatives of the Land Grant Colleges, State Universities and libraries all pushed for support of their institutions in the first batch of proposals to be funded. It was judged important to 'set the tone'.

The Department of Commerce, which had responsibility for the program, eventually funded proposals which seemed to be a compromise between innovative and more traditional activities. It then devoted its efforts to developing new proposals, which would take points of view different from those of earlier proposals, and to monitoring which would make the universities live up to what they had said they would do.

In the meantime, there arose the problem of finding a permanent director for the program. The conflict of agency interests surrounding it made the position seem precarious to many of those to whom it was offered. Eventually, it went to one of the more attractive candidates put forward by the Land Grant College association. Over a period of two to three years, most of those originally associated with the generation of the program had left the Department, and there was a marked reduction of the tension between those proposing and those disposing.

In this example, we can see a number of principles at work.

The processes of forming and implementing policy were both political processes, in which national and local interests expressed themselves. The constellation of those interests and powers set the framework within which the propose-dispose process took place. The effort to establish innovative policy met the resistance of established institutions, some of which tried to defeat the program and others to co-opt it. Because of the tortuous process of policy formation, which required many interconnected steps of approval and reformulation, and because federal agencies were swayed by powerful forces outside the government, established institutions were able to build their interests into the policy itself and into the mechanisms of implementation. When the policy came to be implemented under the propose-dispose model, these same interests re-expressed themselves in the proposals of local agencies. It was as though these interests had been compressed in the policy and expanded again in the process of implementation.

Under these conditions, the propose-dispose model lends itself to a kind of game. Central and local agencies take different roles and perspectives. For central, the propose-dispose process is a means of selecting local agents and stamping in behavior congruent with central policy. For the local agents, the process is a ritual performed in order to get money to carry out their own objectives.

There is always a tendency for federal funds to be drawn away from the goals of central policy and toward the actual goals of local agencies. And there is a countertendency on the part of central to force the funds back into channels conforming to central policy.

Within such a framework, there are predictable moves and counter-moves available both to central and local agencies.

◆ Central

> Set up a competition among local agencies, among regions, among individuals, so as to increase central power of selection and action.
>
> Conceal the amount of funds available, so as to heighten the competition.
>
> Employ independent people to evaluate and monitor the local agents, so that they act as levers on them.
>
> Employ the threat of cancellation or non-funding. This must stop short of the point when a substantial number of subjects become unwilling to play (after all, if they all stop playing, central loses).

◆ Local

> Propose what central wants to hear, but do what you want to do.
>
> Develop a rhetoric compatible with central policy.
>
> Play funding agencies off against one another.
>
> Seek minimum federal control over the use of money.
>
> Take advantage of a surplus of information about what is going on at the local level, and the high cost of finding out for central.
>
> Bring pressure to bear on the funding agency, exploiting its political insecurities.
>
> Attempt to gain central's commitment over time, so that it develops a heavy investment in the local venture and finds it difficult to back out.

Broad new central policy is not applicable, *per se*, to many dispersed localities. There are real differences between the perspectives and interests of local agents. Further, the very process by which new central policy comes into good currency makes it lag behind local perceptions of real issues. Where the relevant situation is changing fast, the first perception of the change is apt to be a local one. The process of central policy formation tends to consist in a compression of diverse and conflicting interests which come unstuck again at the local level. Each policy then becomes a projective test for local representatives of divergent interests, each of which sees in the policy what is enhancing or threatening to it. Finally, central has a vested interest in seeing that policy is implemented uniformly, since this permits its administrative mechanisms to work, whereas the essence of local interests is diversity.

The disparities between central and local agent which undermine the propose-dispose mode of implementing policy have their roots in the same sorts of disparities which cause the failure of center-periphery systems for the diffusion of innovations. To these inherent distortions central may contribute confusing specifications of policy, reflecting incompletely resolved conflicts of agency interests. Or central may monitor in a way that increases the evasive action practiced at the local level, so that more and more of the available energy goes into the attempt to exercise, and then to escape, control.

If the argument to this point is sound, it follows that the other models of central implementation of policy will not escape these distorting forces. So long as the model assumes the prior establishment of central policy which is to be spread uniformly through local systems, distortions will arise in practice.

◆   The models which do not monitor or impose sanctions may avoid the investment of energy in game-playing, but may yield inaction.

◆   The legal model may yield no change, least change or a game of efforts at compulsion and evasion.

◆   The extension of central organizations into the periphery may simply internalize the conflicts between central and regional elements.

The example of the State Technical Services Program displayed some of the pathologies of the rational, center-periphery model. The following example suggests an alternative approach to policy implementation.

The Regional Medical Program

In the mid-1960s a Federal Commission, headed by the Houston surgeon, Michael DeBakey, proposed the initiation of a national program devoted to heart disease, cancer, and stroke—sometimes called the 'Congressional diseases'. Central to the program was the notion that advances in medical technology—for example, open heart surgery and intensive coronary care—had not spread beyond the great medical centers. The Commission wished to promote their equitable distribution.

To this end, it adopted what came to be known as the DeBakey model, a system for the regionalization of medical care which linked to every center of medical teaching and research a periphery of community hospitals and practising physicians. Through the dissemination of information, continuing education, training, and the deployment of specialized facilities for care, new medical technology was to flow outward from the medical center. The role of 'central' was to distribute resources (about 100 million dollars), and to oversee and control the diffusion of the DeBakey model throughout fifty-five medical 'regions'.

From this starting point, two sets of consequences ensued.

1 The actual goals of the local regions turned out to be different from central's. The regions were 'discovered

systems' with their own interests and their own styles of interaction, regardless of the purposes central assigned to them. The regions were interested, for example, in supporting local medical schools, compensating for a decline in medical research funding, and securing continuing resources for programs already established. Key actors in the regions were concerned with their own survival in their positions, with independence of action, with local conditions and needs (as opposed to central's view of them), with the protection and extension of their territories, and with the maintenance of local stability.

Under these conditions, the familiar game began to be played in which what central saw as an opportunity for shaping local behavior, local agencies saw as a way of capturing central resources for their own ends.

2 This separation of the central manager's system and the discovered systems of the regions had its consequences for evaluation.

When the two systems have little overlap and little interaction, evaluation is limited to retrospective justification. In this condition, the evaluation system produces statements believed neither by producer nor by the consumer ('We have established a regionalized medical technology transfer system') which are generated ritualistically in response to formal demand. Central demands a verbal indication of regional conformity with central policy, and the discovered system of the region responds by 'conning'. The two systems operate substantially in parallel, implicitly agreed not to disturb or influence one another.

Where central presses the regions for more concrete instances of conformity to central policy, the discovered systems of the regions may respond by adapting to the prescribed measures of performance but otherwise carrying on as much as possible as before. Central can evaluate and control only through measures, but the measures are always distinguishable from the desired performance

itself. So RMPs provided information on 'numbers of
nurses trained' or 'numbers of physicians subscribed in
courses'.

In an analogous effort at evaluation and control, Congress once pressed the Vocational Rehabilitation system
to indicate how many 'rehabilitations per year' the
agency effected for a given investment. 'Rehabilitations'
were defined as placings in jobs lasting three months or
more. As a consequence, the Vocational Rehabilitation
system began to 'cream' its clientele for those most likely
to find jobs, leaving out those who were most in need and
least able to qualify; it began to select low-level jobs for
graduates so as to make it easier for them to get accepted;
systematically to avoid distinguishing between a 'case'
and a person, so that a graduate who had been given a
job, lost it and returned to training, could be counted as
another 'rehabilitation'; and systematically to avoid
follow-up of clients after three months.

But the discovered systems of the regions were by no
means entirely negative in their effects. Some coordinators were beginning to use the Regional Medical Program
to help solve what they saw as the local problems of the
medical care system of the region. They saw the medical
care system mismatched to need and unable to respond
because of manpower shortages, the attitudes of the professions, and the fragmentation of a system whose elements are not under the control of any single person or
agency.

In some of the regions, coordinators devoted themselves primarily to the sorts of changes in institutional
arrangements which, from the point of view of the De-
Bakey model, figured only as a means to an end. For
them, RMP dealt with an overall improvement in the
quality and accessibility of care. This required changes
in the structure and interaction of the institutions concerned, so as to 'knit together components of the system'.

For example,

◆ In one State, the coordinator used the problem of purchasing and distributing new facilities for coronary care as an occasion for inducing thirteen community hospitals to undertake a broad-ranging process of joint purchasing and planning.

◆ In North Carolina, the coordinator used the program to connect the medically rich resources of Raleigh-Durham with the medically poor back counties of the State.

◆ In New Jersey, the coordinator managed to get several of the large, urban medical centers to take on responsibility for medical care in the urban ghettoes in which they lived, but which they had previously ignored.

In short, some of the coordinators began to use RMP as a vehicle for transforming the medical care systems of their regions.

In the meantime, certain changes were occurring at the national level. There had been a movement into good currency of certain basic concerns about the national system for providing medical care—concerns about rising medical costs, about the effective exclusion from the health care system of large numbers of disadvantaged people, about shortages of medical manpower, about the difficulties of negotiating the medical care system even for ordinary middle-class people. The effect of substantial investment in Medicare and Medicaid had begun to convince observers that no amount of investment in payment for care would suffice to introduce necessary changes in the system providing it. Clearly, there had to be intervention on the provider side as well. Yet there were overriding objections both to the development of nationalized systems of care and to the widespread use of decentralized solutions such as community-based group practice. Shortages of medical manpower suggested that efforts to

change the system would have to use existing personnel
and, very largely, existing institutions. This meant trying
to foster voluntary rearrangements of existing institutions. And of the available programs that might be used
to bring this about, RMP seemed perhaps the most promising candidate.

RMP-central responded, then, not by punishing the
'deviant' coordinators but by beginning to reformulate
central policy. 'Transformation of the system of medical
care' began to become the central concept of the program. But from this, several things followed:

◆ There was no model for systems transformation
   which could be spread uniformly over the regions.
   Each region had its own starting conditions, and
   presented its own special problems.

◆ Each regional process had to be regarded as essentially open-ended. It could not impose a medical
   care system on the region. It had to be committed
   to engaging the emerging issues of medical care,
   whatever these turned out to be.

Central's role, therefore, had to shift. It could enunci-
ate *themes* of policy—'transformation of the medical care
system,' 'equity of access to care'—but it could not formulate and impose a program for adoption by the regions.
On the contrary, the generation of central policy had to
be *inductively* derived from the regions. Regions developed
variations on central themes.

There could therefore be no central evaluation of regional performance. But central could provide 'meta'
evaluation of the regions—that is, it could require that
the regions generate their own developing policies for
change, and that *they* devise and use systems of evaluation which would permit them to justify, control, and
learn from what they were doing. Moreover, central
could connect regions with one another to produce what

was, in effect, a network for learning about transformation of the medical care system.

Implementation of policy in a learning system

The problem of implementing policy in a learning context is the problem of setting in motion and guiding, around central policy themes, a network of related processes of local public learning.

Within this process, the formation of policy cannot be neatly separated from its implementation. Every alleged example of local implementation of central policy, if it results in significant social transformation, is in fact a process of local social discovery. After-the-fact, there may be a way to state the new social policy to which all the local discoveries conform. But before the fact, there is no single policy statement which can be used to induce them.

Hence, the fostering of these processes cannot take the form of pre-defining policy and causing it to fan out from a center. Central may provide first instances or policy themes which are take-off points for chains of transformation in localities. It may help local agencies to learn from one another's experience. It may even lend its weight to shifts in power structure which seem likely to lead to social discovery at the local level.

Also, the transformations of local systems influence one another, and may be supported in doing so. Moreover, the gradual transformation of the system as a whole influences the context in which each local system experiences its own transformation. The broad process can 'go critical' as ideas underlying the family of transformations come into good currency and as the numbers of learners and extenders multiply.

A system capable of behaving in this manner is a learning system. Within it, central's role is that of initiator, facilitator and goad to local learning. Such a process comes inevitably into conflict with demands for

stable adherence to specific policies, and with demands
for uniformity in the application of policies. It comes inevitably into conflict with many traditional procedures
of the legislative and administrative process. It places
special demands on the social systems of the agencies and
on the networks through which information, people and
money flow from central to local agencies and from all
of these to one another.

IV   Government as a social system

We have so far concentrated on functions of government
essential to public learning, processes by which issues and
ideas emerge as powerful for action, processes by which
policy comes to be implemented. But government is more
than a series of functions. It is also a social system built
around those functions, and its characteristics as a society
determine its ability to engage in public learning.

It is a negative but by no means entirely inaccurate
characterization of government agencies to say that they
are memorials to old problems. From this point of view
the Department of Agriculture is an organizational edi-
fice constructed around the problems of agricultural productivity as they appeared in the United States in the
latter part of the nineteenth century. The fundamental
solution of these problems, to the point of creating new
problems of agricultural surplus, did not lead to the
passing away of the Department of Agriculture but to its
expansion; there are still 70,000 agricultural extension
agents operating in the field in the United States.

The Department of Labor came into being around the
problems of unemployment and labor conflict as they
arose in the 1930s. The solution of these problems, or the
development of independent institutions dedicated to
their solution, has not led to the disappearance of the
Department of Labor but again to its extension. The
Department of Commerce is an accretion of new organizational structures added to old ones; its growth process

is organic and results in products like the stratified layers of shells. The Small Business Administration is a monument to Congressional nostalgia for the 'little man who made it', even though his entrepreneurial role in American industry no longer has the status or importance it once had.

The general rule is that agencies come into being and assume their form in response to specific national problems and crises. When the problems and crises disappear or change drastically in nature, the old organizational structure persists. The actual physical structure of Washington, with its layers of buildings in varying architectural styles, is a symbol of this organizational process. In government, as in most other established institutions, the organizational equivalent of biological death is missing.

Words such as 'inertia' or 'bureaucratic stagnation' or 'resistance to change' are not particularly helpful in explaining this process. As with other dynamically conservative societies, it is essential to understand the ways in which government agencies provide for their members a basis for security, not only a secure job but a necessary feeling of place and belonging. The agency provides a focus for loyalty, a definition of role, a sense of identity, an upward path through which progress and promotion are defined, and a perspective on the world. The concept of agency as a functionally autonomous society, responding to the most deeply felt needs of its members, helps to explain something of the vital persistence of agency structure and organization in the face of shifts in the character of the situation which brought that agency into being. Even the language used in the agencies helps to make this clear. I have always been struck by the number of different agencies in which 'the bureau' has only one meaning and 'the director' refers only to one man.

Units of organization differ, of course, in the extent to which they are deeply rooted in these social functions.

In the Department of Commerce, for example, the Bureau of Standards and the Bureau of the Census, the Coast and Geodetic Survey, and the Weather Bureau are particularly notable in this regard. Membership in these organizations carries with it connection to a tradition which provides both values for judging the outside world (for example, the critical importance of values attaching to measurement, precision, detachment, objectivity, scientific method and fairness) and a sense of the importance of one's own role. Personnel policies, like those defining tenure for civil servants, do not create organizational loyalty and organization persistence; they merely provide the legal and institutional counterpart of the social function.

Government agencies are societies that display special forms of dynamic conservatism. One need only reflect on the feelings of a member of an agency bureaucracy who has been in government sufficiently long to feel committed to it as a career and to see retirement benefits as his principal form of financial security. If he has lived in the agency for a period of ten years or more, he is likely to have seen at least five changes of chief. How do you respond when you are a member of an organization whose head keeps being chopped off? An entire array of strategies and life styles has grown up to permit survival at minimum cost and in some instances to protect determined persistence at productive work. The strategies include probing the character, intentions and sophistication of the new incumbent; currying favor in a new program; internal sales; re-casting in terms of new programs the activities to which one has long been committed; search for the tall grass in which to remain impervious to attention; ways of giving the boss what he wants with minimum disturbance of ongoing activity. There are in a number of government agencies individuals of high intelligence and great dedication, whose only means of persisting in work on problems they judge to be of national importance is a kind of guerilla warfare through which this work is either bootlegged, hidden, or recast continually to meet the perceived requirements of new temporary chiefs.

In addition, the relationship of agencies to one another is best characterized as a conflict of rival baronies, each jealously guarding its own territory and seeking to expand that territory at the expense of other agencies. No new program moves into the Federal Government as into a neutral space but always into a field of force built out of the territorial fears and ambitions of the agencies. These persist from administration to administration, have a life-cycle that is longer than that of any given administration, and while influenced by the activities of an administration, lead a life of their own. As a result, it sometimes appears to an outside observer that the Federal Government contains many extremely intelligent, highly dedicated, experienced individuals who work long hours over long periods of time cancelling one another out.

Given these characteristics of the system of agency societies, what happens when a new national problem emerges? (That is to say, when an old national problem comes into good currency and presents itself, through processes which have been suggested in an earlier section, as a fit subject for federal action.)

Within the last two federal administrations, examples of such problems are the following:

- The decay of the city

- Pollution of land, sea and air

- Relations between universities and their surrounding communities

- Regional economic development

- The problems of industrial work generally grouped under the heading of 'automation'

◆ The handling of scientific and technical information

◆ The problems of assessing national requirements for manpower and of developing manpower adequate to those needs.[11]

When a problem of this kind is discovered and comes under consideration, it usually reveals a highly fragmented picture in which every major agency owns a piece of the problem. I remember a conversation between Luther Hodges and a number of his aides when Hodges was Secretary of Commerce. The conversation began with the problem of water resources. One of the aides said: 'We have been looking into the matter and it looks to us as though there are about twenty agencies involved in water resource development.' Another said: 'That's strange, we have been concerned with pollution control, and there are about twenty agencies involved in that.' Hodges offered the opinion that this was perhaps because, after all, there were about twenty major agencies.

The problem of the cities belongs in the Federal Housing Administration because of its special concern with urban housing. It belongs in the Department of Commerce because of the role of the cities in economic development. It belongs in the Department of Health, Education and Welfare because of the city as a focus for health, education and welfare services. It belongs in the Department of Agriculture because the city consumes the nation's agricultural products. It belongs in the Department of Interior because the city is a center for the consumption, distribution, and use of natural resources. Moreover, every major agency turns out to be undertaking programs which relate in some direct fashion, or which can be interpreted as relating, to urban problems. The same is true with respect to every major problem listed above.

As a new federal problem is identified, such fragmentation comes to light.[12] And there is apt to be at the same time the beginnings of in-fighting over territory. At this point, there are several alternative strategies available to an administration that wishes to launch a major attack on the problem:

1 Establish an inter-agency committee whose function is to coordinate and jointly manage the various agency activities relating to the problem area. Such a committee can be defined with a weak role, such as that of keeping track of or monitoring activities, or it can be given a strong role relating, for example, to the development of standards of agency performance, or even to the co-ordination of inter-agency activity. I have participated in about six inter-agency committees with durations of one year or more, and as a matter of interest have enquired of other individuals who have also participated in them, whether anyone has been a member of such a committee which was effective in carrying out the functions assigned it. I have never received an affirmative answer. The committee may make a show of performance during the early stages of its operation and particularly if it is subject to some strong external threat (as the inter-agency committee on scientific information was, for example, during the early sixties). But shortly, usually within a matter of months, the principal forces at work appear to be those of individual agency baronies and the demands of territoriality. The actual, as opposed to the official agenda, becomes that of assuring and protecting the territorial interests of each agency, rather than that of cooperatively attacking the problems which lie in inter-agency space. Given what has been said about the function of the agency as a society, the territorial relationships among agencies and the permanence of underlying bureaucracies compared to the transience of political administrations, this should be by no means surprising.

2 Another strategy is that of a consolidating reorganization. The establishment of the Department of Housing and Urban Development is such a case. So is the recent establishment within the Department of Health, Education and Welfare of the Social Rehabilitation Agency, bringing together independent groups such as Vocational Rehabilitation, Welfare, Children's Bureau and the like. In a smaller way, so was the establishment within the Department of Commerce in the early sixties of the Environmental Science Survey agency and the reorganization of the Bureau of Standards. The success of such reorganizations depends greatly on whether or not they are accompanied by a large infusion of new funds. If not, they are apt to consist of the simple coalition of operating units with a thin layer of coordinating administration and a new rhetoric of function, which usually exceeds by a great deal the actual ability of the agency to perform. The temptation is to continue to perform the old functions in the old way under new headings. An active administration will attempt to impose new activities and to revitalize old structures, and will find itself engaged in a complicated bargaining process with the heads of subunits.

3 Still another strategy is the creation of a new organization dedicated to work on the new problem. The Peace Corps and the Office of Economic Opportunity are both examples. The new organization can bring an infusion of new vitality, new faces and enthusiasm to new programs. The organization may be loose and informal and the morale and spirit high. Its problems will arise from the process of bureaucratic aging—a kind of life cycle. The problems of the aging process, for example, are what the Peace Corps, after about five years, seems now to be principally concerned with, despite the interesting invention of the 'five-year flush' as a way of preserving vitality. The current problems of the Tennessee Valley Authority are similar, though working over a

longer term. A characteristic pattern is that in which one administration will take a new problem and a new agency under its wing, provide it with special attention and a boss of character and energy, giving it unusual freedoms within the bureaucratic system and encouraging a climate of high morale and creativity. Over time, the specially protected character of the agency will fade away, bureaucratic restrictions will arise once again and encroach upon its territory, internal divisions will tend to rigidify, the original entrepreneur of the agency will leave, and a new chief of lesser originality and with fewer degrees of freedom in which to operate will take over.

This is, to some extent, a pattern characteristic of the creation of every new agency within the Federal Government. What one would like to achieve is very much like what every large-scale organization within our society would also like to achieve: a way of adapting flexibly to the emergence of new problems, discarding old structures as they become inappropriate and vestigial, and changing the character of approach, use of personnel and allocation of resources to suit new tasks as they arise.

Approaches to this sort of adaptation can be analyzed under the heading of 'self-renewing organizations' (where the shift to work on new problems can be accomplished within the boundaries of an existing organization) or under the heading of new forms of inter-agency organization.

A great deal has been written about the problems of designing self-renewing organizations.[13] Real accomplishment along these lines appears still to be marginal. Nevertheless, a number of relevant points can be made, some broadly applicable to all established organizations, some peculiar to the Federal Government.

◆ A great deal of the problem of organizational renewal has to do with the opening up of boundaries —both those of compartments within agencies and those separating agencies from the outside world. The oldest and most static Federal agencies are those with the most air-tight organizational compartments—originally related to function but often, in the course of time, of unclear or irrelevant function. Horizontal movement across compartments becomes unthinkable. Similarly, static agencies are relatively isolated from the outside world— from other agencies of government, from broader communities.

The opening up of boundaries—through the breaking down or restructuring of internal barriers, enforced movement across barriers, and the infusion of new blood—tends to threaten not only established patterns of organization but also established ways of seeing the world and established ideologies tied to organizational form. This is true particularly of parochial views of the world (concern *only* with the department and its business) and of ideologies based on fear of 'the others' (the department as a bastion against the outside world).

◆ 'Young Turks' occupy a critical position. An agency head can revitalize his organization by attracting new bright young people, placing them in positions of unusual access to policy and program guidance (for example, by creating special 'assistant' and 'aide' positions), by designing training programs that expose young people to views from the top and confront departmental heads with their challenges. Informal organizations of young people—across divisional or hierarchical boundaries—can strengthen their role. One agency head has recently constructed an agency of young people, counterpart to his own, to develop counterpart agency programs and policies and to formulate and test out pilot projects.

◆ Characteristically, there develop among federal agencies informal networks that can realistically be called 'undergrounds'. These are groups of individuals attracted to the idea of change in agency policy and practice, and committed to the use of the informal system to effect that change. Such undergrounds may be used—as indicated earlier—to preserve continuity of effort underneath a changing pattern of agency heads. They may also represent guerilla movements aimed at changing agency policy and, sometimes, at subverting official policy to other ends.

Occasionally, agency heads ally themselves with the underground, in order to force change through layers of official bureaucracy or to by-pass their own official structures.

Again, informal connections may be established across agency lines, sometimes through individuals who serve as the nodes of these informal systems. Coalitions form around efforts to change particular policies, or movements are started to take advantage of crises to introduce change.

Because most formal interagency measures fail, informal networks are often the chief means by which agencies can be coordinated in working on new problems that cut across their boundaries.

◆ New views of national problems, and of the role of the federal government, tend to form around individual leaders, and to be identified with them. But these leaders come and go. Their 'time constant' is usually shorter than that of the agencies in which they function, and shorter than the period needed to follow through the programs they have helped to define. Hence, one always has to consider how credible the leaders are to the more permanent middle levels of bureaucracy who will

finally take responsibility for the critically important implementation of programs.[14]

Further, the introduction of new program ideas
tends to be accompanied, in a new administration,
by sharp and frequently shifting political pressures
for performance *now*. The effect is often to paralyze
or demoralize the middle levels of the agency, who
come to feel that they are unable to build anything.

The credibility of leaders has a great deal to do
with their ability to protect those below from
shifting and destructive pressures for immediate
(and often contradictory) response. This protection
may come from the interest of the President, who
gives the program special treatment (as FDR did
for the TVA and Kennedy did for the Peace Corps)
or from the political strength and skill of the agency
head himself.

◆ All of these measures and approaches represent
ways of loosening up an agency so that it can address itself creatively to new problems. But the renewal may be a one-shot effort, lasting no longer
than the tenure of a particular leader or of a particular administration. These measures do not of
themselves ensure that the agency will continue to
be capable of renewing itself, and attempts are
sometimes made to build that capability into the
structure of the institution.

From one point of view, the Planning, Programming and Budgeting System (PPBS), fostered by
the Bureau of the Budget and based on techniques
introduced by Secretary McNamara into the Department of Defense, is an attempt to institutionalize the capability for continuing renewal. It seeks
to force agencies to define programs in functional
terms, which permit alternative designs for accom-
plishing those functions; to develop ways of asses-

sing the outcome which systematically confront the agency's intent with its actual accomplishment; and to budget by function. But it has become clear that PPBS by itself cannot serve this end. The technique may force reconsideration of agency policies and may provide opportunities for those interested in change to move towards new definitions of programs. Equally, the PPBS may simply repackage old programs, without making a real change in function or organization.

Attempts to institutionalize the informal systems of agencies seem to embody a contradiction: the very vitality of informal systems depends on their informal status, their invisibility.

Opening up the boundaries of organizations, fostering the influx of young people, are measures with finite lives. They are not self-sustaining.

The tendency is for agencies to seek new stable states, coalescing around the modified programs, organizational structures, views of the world and ideologies that have resulted from the last infusion of innovation.

When the new problem does not lie easily within the boundaries of an established agency, flexible adaptation demands a response different from the self-defeating or time-limited responses listed earlier. If the question is how to produce not a one-shot response but a continuing adaptation, then one useful and evocative image is that of a structure made up of pools of competence and task forces. The characteristics of such an organization are these:

♦ Pools of competence are organized around disciplines or skills. These may be in the nature of 'content' skills—statistics, computer programming, accounting, economics, social service, engineering—

or 'process skills' such as planning, program management, coordination. These skills must be relevant to the demands of federal program and policy, and available when government requires them.

The managers of these pools are in a sense gardeners who are concerned with making good use of people, training and retraining them, keeping continuity of professional development, putting the right man in the right job, forming task-groups and returning the men in them into competence pools, and (most important) providing a basis for professional security throughout a period of changing tasks.

Ideally the objective of such an organization would be to develop a sense of identity and loyalty to it and to the objectives of the Federal Government, rather than to specific agencies or bureaus.[15]

◆   On the other hand, there would be a series of task groups responsible for specific projects. These would have shorter life cycles than competence pools. Members of competence pools would move in and out of task groups, in the manner of project management systems in individual firms. Projects would be managed so as to achieve their goals according to given criteria of performance and cost.

◆   Such a system requires an intelligence function which identifies requirements for new projects and determines the effect of ongoing activity; and a control function which monitors projects, presses for modification and determines the life-cycles of the projects. Both are part of a system of program management which organizes projects into coherent, connected wholes.

Clearly, such an approach is inappropriate to management of the routine functions of government, to the relatively standard performance of tasks with long life-cycles like those performed by the Bureau of the Census, the Post Office, the Bureau of Labor Statistics, and the like. Even these functions have life-cycles, however—as indicated by the current crisis in postal operations.

Such an approach *is* appropriate to the management of new functions of government which are non-routine and have relatively short (though not precisely predictable) life cycles. In this respect, the model of a Federal 'project system' represents in the area of program management what has already become familiar and frequently effective in the realm of deliberation, evaluation and planning. The use of Federal task forces, commissions and planning groups, has become a commonplace. Task forces have been formed on problems of the cities, on crime, on children, on the problem of privacy. At any given time, their number probably is in the hundreds. They have limited lives. They are called into being by the President or by heads of offices and agencies. Their members are drawn from other organizations, Federal or non-Federal, and return to those organizations when their tasks are completed. The 'project system' model would carry over to program management an approach now broadly applied to the analysis of problems and the evaluation of programs.

The creation of new agencies like the Office of Economic Opportunity or the Peace Corps does not fit the model. Its failure to do so hinges principally on the issue of security.

People are attracted to new agencies both from old agencies and from business organizations and universities, as well as from local government, labor and the social services. Upon the disbanding of an agency (an event frequently discussed, but almost never undertaken) people could find their way into other agencies of government or filter back into the non-governmental sector. But there are no provisions for such a transition. If no organizational home is in prospect, disbanding comes to seem threatening and disruptive. The prevailing expectation is that the agency will survive. In order to bolster the expectation, members of a new agency quickly learn the bureaucratic survival game, which requires identifying, linking to and serving constituencies powerful enough to insure the permanence of the agency. Examples are the Department of Agriculture's constituencies among extension agents and the extension departments of Land Grant Colleges, and the Department of Labor's constituencies within organized labor.

A federal project system would need to foster security through other means, by creating continuing pools of competence to which its members *expect* to return when their tasks are completed. There is a recent model in the 'in-and-outer' who moves from the university or foundation to government, and back again with a change in political fortunes, with the completion of a job, or simply with fatigue. This is again an informal network and one that works, by and large, only for an elite. No comparable arrangements exist for the lower and middle level employees and it is they who are left to carry on.

In spite of some relevant industrial examples, the form and location of competence pools and the techniques of management appropriate to them remain to be invented. The model, however, suggests a direction in which to seek the organizational flexibility required by the changing character of national problems.

Conclusion

Government is an institution for performing public functions and an agent for inquiring into public problems affecting society as a whole.

As an instrument of public learning, the federal government of the United States rests largely on a theory of the stable state. It accepts as mysteriously given the issues around which policy and program must be shaped. It treats government as center, the rest of society as periphery. Central has responsibility for the formation of new policy and for its imposition on localities at the periphery. Central attempts to 'train' agencies at the periphery. In spite of the language of experimentation, government-initiated learning tends to be confined to efforts to induce localities to behave in conformity with central policy. Localities learn to beat the system. Government tends to bury failure or to learn from it only in the sense of veering away from it. Evaluation, then, tends to be limited to the role of establishing and monitoring the extent of peripheral conformity with central policy.

The social systems of the agencies mirror the theory underlying the implementation of policies. Agencies are the social embodiment of policies, and in their efforts to sustain and protect themselves they also sustain and protect established policy. New problems fragment established agencies just as they fragment established policies. With the loss of the stable state, policies must be viewed as transient, their change being the foreground condition, and continuing fragmentation of agencies and policies becoming the rule.

For government to become a learning system, both the social system of agencies and the theory of policy implementation must change. Government cannot play the role of 'experimenter for the nation', seeking first to identify the correct solution, then to train society at large in its adaptation. The opportunity for learning is primarily in discovered systems at the periphery, not in the nexus of official policies at the center. Central's role is to detect significant shifts at the periphery, to pay explicit attention to the emergence of ideas in good currency, and to derive themes of policy by induction. The movement of learning is as much from periphery to periphery, or from periphery to center, as from center to periphery.

Central comes to function as facilitator of society's learning, rather than as society's trainer.

Such a role is not appropriate to the stable areas of society in which steady, routine functions of government continue to be carried out; but it is appropriate to the areas in which public learning is required. Such a role deprives central of its monopoly on the formation of new policy. It demands a shift in the social system of government, which now serves and reinforces stable, compartmentalized policy. The concept of a government 'project system', made up of task forces and competence pools, serves only to illustrate what government as a self-transforming system might become.

When applied to government, this view of learning raises serious problems:

- The concept of legislation as a basis for policy tends to be accompanied by commitment to policy which remains stable over long periods of time. This view of public learning threatens established patterns of legislation, as well as processes for generating legislation and for relationships between administrative and legislative agencies.

- Arguments for the uniform application of policy (a phrase easier to state than to define) often rest on concepts of equity. What is the likelihood that the network of systems transformations at the periphery will result in policies which are equitable from region to region?

- Central government has as one of its functions the correction of inequities practiced in the regions— a function dependent, ostensibly, on its greater leverage and on its distance from the interests of established power in the regions. How is this function compatible with central's facilitative role?

These issues are real and they go to the roots of our

governmental system. There may, indeed, be a conflict between the demands of public learning and the demands of legislative stability and governmental equity. If so, it is a conflict we must meet head on.

♦ 6 Learning systems

I *Two themes*

Under the general rubric of learning systems, we have explored the evolution of business firms, systems for the diffusion of innovation, and clues to the nature of government as a vehicle for public learning. Two themes have played major roles in each of the cases examined: the emergence of functional systems as the units around which institutions define themselves, and the decline of center-periphery models of institutional activity. Not surprisingly, these themes turn out to have common origins and to reinforce one another in their development.

The primacy of functional systems

At any given time, the institutional cross-section of a society reveals a design for addressing the functions which have been thought worth carrying out and for solving the problems thought to be worth solving.

Government agencies grew up around the need to make agriculture more productive, the problems of unemployment in the thirties, the potential for cheap electric power in the Tennessee Valley. Industrial firms organized around functions like papermaking, bridge construction, the transportation of passengers from city to city; and social welfare agencies organized around the rehabilitation of the blind, the treatment of alcoholics and the problems of runaway children.

The institutional map of a society, like the physical map, reflects a process of social design—though organizations seldom if ever take their final form from a single act of design; normally they grow into their identities. Also, their evolution depends upon a rigorous selection from all the characteristics of their prospective clienteles, activities and situations, which in their nature can never be fully enumerated.

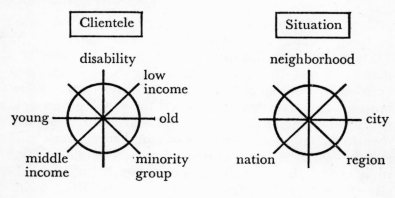

The design of a social welfare agency

Through such a selection process, organizations come to be defined at varying levels of specificity. There is, for example, in the United States a National Council on

Youth and Delinquency, a national agency concerned with youth and narcotics, and an agency serving delinquent, drug-addicted youths in the city of Boston.

In our society, the institutional map displays, in the foreground, organizations defined at high levels of specificity. More general functional systems exist, as it were, only in the background; no individual existing organizations correspond to them. In the foreground is the textile company, the lumber firm, or the hospital; in the background is the system for keeping clothes clean, the building industry, or the health care system.

Over time, we shift our perspectives on the problems that need solving. But institutions have an inertial life of their own; consequently there are always mismatches between the institutional map and the problems thought worth solving. There are always Agriculture Departments offering extension services found to be irrelevant, and industrial firms manufacturing products for which there is declining demand. On the other hand, there are always problems like the problems of the cities which seem to cry out for solution even though no agency corresponds to them.

With the loss of the stable state, this condition of mismatch becomes endemic and universal. There is always a state of mismatch between the institutional map and the array of problems taken to be important.

The diagnosis of the mismatch is itself a social phenomenon, varying with the times. Recently, as we have become aware of the very nearly universal mismatch of organizations to problems, we have begun to formulate the mismatch at higher levels of generality. We see the mismatch not only at the level of the hospital, but at the level of the health care system. Just as, in solving personal problems, it is often helpful to redefine the problem in a more general way (to see the problem, for example, as the design of a fastener rather than a nail), so in the realm of social design we see that we cannot resolve mismatches at any level short of broad functional systems.

But in our society public learning has been limited to the transformation of specific organizations. Broad functional systems transform themselves through slow and uncertain chain reactions. As a consequence of 'wash-and-wear' and 'coin-ops', the system for keeping clothes clean transformed itself. But its transformation was of a kind that no one foresaw, guided, or particularly wanted. Once the mismatch between institutions and problems comes to be perceived in a very general way, we come to realize that we need to raise the level of generality at which we can engage in public learning.

These considerations throw another light on invasion and insurgency, modes of intervention which necessarily limit their targets to established institutions. One cannot very well invade or overthrow an institution that has no embodiment. Invasion and insurgency are insufficient as modes of intervention not merely because they threaten perpetual disruption in an era of loss of the stable state, but because the formation of a new functional system requires, but is not reducible to, battles with established organizations.

The creation of a new, functional system combining many previously separate components leads chiefly to two fundamentally different strategies:

- ◆ Gain control of all elements of the functional system in order to subject them to central management.

- ◆ Knit together the still autonomous elements of the functional system in networks which permit concerted action.

The first is the strategy of a business system firm. It is also the strategy of centralist approaches to the provision of services, like the centrally managed Polyclinics of the

Soviet health system. The second strategy recommends itself when political, economic or managerial considerations make it impossible to internalize all the elements of a functional system. Examples of the second exist under headings like 'facilitation', 'coordination', and 'knitting together'.

Both strategies bring new networks into being—in the first case, networks internal to the framework of single organization; in the second, networks of semi-autonomous elements. In both cases, the strategies create new problems in the design, development and management of networks.

The argument to this point carries with it a number of corollaries:

- However the elements of a new functional system are connected, their organization must take on the character of a temporary, fluid system, comparable to the 'project system' of government or to the shifting internal organization of the 'Movement'. The loss of the stable state carries with it continuing mismatch between specific elements and their situations, and thereby precipitates movement up the ladder of functional aggregation—that is, it tends to make organizations define their functions in more and more encompassing terms.

  The importance of this movement is not that it permits once-and-for-all redesign of institutions but that it permits continual redesign of organizational elements within the framework of broad functional systems. Hence, the need for an internal organization which can be continually redesigned without flying apart at the seams.

- Within the system, the foreground condition is not stability but change. Attention focuses on the process of transforming one structure into another rather than on the resulting structure. 'Around here,' members of established organizations sometimes say, 'it's one damn reorganization after another.' But within a functional system that is a learning system, internal restructuring comes to be seen not as an aberration but as the norm. Emotion and energy which previously went into the maintenance of a stable structure come to be invested in the process of transformation.

◆ When conditions cannot be forecast far ahead, the need for continuing internal transformation puts a high priority on responsiveness to new information. This means a priority on fast footwork and short turn-around times, and on the ability to detect new issues, and to perceive the mismatch between ideas in good currency and realities within the discovered system.

◆ Nevertheless, it still remains essential for organizations to give their members security. Individuals still look to them for a sense of their role and identity, for perspectives on the world, and for relief from uncertainty. Dynamic conservatism cannot be expected to disappear. But just as there is a shift upward in the level of aggregation at which the organization defines itself, so there must be a shift upward in the level at which the organization provides security and identity for its members. The sense of membership moves from specific elements in the organization to functional systems.

◆ With the new strategies of institutional design, new roles come into prominence. In an era of instability, roles of intervention become more prominent than roles of stability; the entrepreneur, invader, organizer, advocate, consultant, muckraker, and the change-oriented leader become more visible and important than those who fill essential roles in steady-state organizations. But with the primacy of functional systems, the prominent roles of intervention take on a special character. They become the roles related to responsiveness to new information (prophet, artist, visionary) and the network roles essential to the design, development and management of the shifting networks on which functional systems depend.

◆ When the sense of need to move to higher levels of functional aggregation does not carry with it the ability to do so, attention shifts to the technologies of network management and design. Hence, the importance of new techniques and styles of management derived from experiences as disparate as aerospace and weapons systems and the history of the movement.

The line of argument about the primacy of functional systems suggests what may seem to be an idle question. How far up the ladder of aggregation is it possible to go? Driven by the pervasiveness of the mismatch between more specific organizational elements and their situations, will we find ways to move up to functional levels we have as yet no way to describe? Many home-builders still find it a new idea, for example, to be part of a housing system. Educators have only recently learned not to be surprised at being parts of an educational system. What concepts lie beyond the 'housing' or 'health' systems whose names, at any rate, have become familiar? Or will society as a whole become the functional unit around which we define organizational identity and to which we look for security?

When we move beyond the concepts of established organizations, options appear. Functional systems are neither pre-made nor fixed. At a level of aggregation which allows institutions to be redesigned on a broad enough scale, there are many possible arrangements of elements corresponding to many possible definitions of function. These options become turning points for the society and subjects of major social conflict. Will we build new systems around vertical functions like housing or health, or will we build multiple and inter-related functional systems around particular regional, geographic, or community units? Will we design comprehensive community systems, more or less independent of one another, or will we design national housing, health and welfare systems, all of which impinge on communities? Or will we find ourselves necessarily having to combine the two?

Our culture seems to be moving in the direction of designing quasi-autonomous functional systems organized around youth and age. Will we persevere in these trends, or will we be caught up in the need to design functional systems which match the scope of society as a whole?

The decline of the center-periphery model

The center-periphery model has been the dominant model in our society for the growth and diffusion of organizations defined at high levels of specificity. For such a system, the uniform, simple message is essential. The system's ability to handle complex situations depends upon a simple message and upon growth through uniform replication.

The mismatch between institutions and problems presents itself in a special light when the institution is in center-periphery form. The center sees mismatch at the periphery as loss of control—heresy, deviationism, or simple insubordination. It may respond by devising a system for detection and punishment or by cutting off the offending peripheral agency.

When the mismatches threaten to become endemic at the periphery, undermining the central message as a whole, central can behave in such a way as to make its message come true. It can induce the emergence of uniform situations to which a uniform message applies. Hence, the self-fulfilling prophecies of authoritarian government: there is treachery and subversion in our midst, let us wipe it out; and by wiping it out we produce in others the behavior we feared. Advertising and merchandising may function in this way: industry must create the classes of uniform wants that its uniform, mass-produced products can satisfy. Schools may create in parents and children the uniform expectations of learning which the center-periphery system of the school can meet. If human situations are not discovered to be uniform in the sense required by the world, they must be made uniform.

All of this provides another perspective on cultural homogenization, a perspective different from those of social critics like Marcuse, Ellul and Goodman. Cultural uniformity is not merely a function of modern technology but of the limits to the informational capacity of center-periphery organizations. Center-periphery systems depend on a stable, relatively simple message which can be spread uniformly over a periphery.[1] Both the excesses of industrially generated cultural uniformity and the excesses of authoritarian repression may be understood as responses to the overwhelming complexity of growth and management in any mode other than center-periphery.

The center-periphery system's self-fulfilling prophecy is a response to the loss of the stable state. But it is a response that often provokes a reaction of its own. The system's pressure for uniformity at the periphery meets counter-pressures for local participation, autonomy, and control by the users. Often these pressures seem to require a total breakdown of central control. Radical decentralism arises in response to the forced uniformity and perceived injustice of center-periphery systems.

But radical decentralism creates as many problems as it solves. The same technological shifts that produce loss of the stable state also connect the pieces of our society with one another. There can be no isolated, autonomous localities. The need is for differentiated, responsive, continually changing but *connected* reaction.

From the point of view of this need, the institutions we have considered as learning systems represent a range of strategies.

The constellation firm permits diversity at the periphery without giving up central control. It converts the center to an entrepreneurial role and the central message to an entrepreneurial process, but the center-periphery structure remains.

That form of governmental process which allows central policy to shift in response to discovered systems at the periphery is an important modification.

But both of these are least-change adaptations. They retain the center-periphery structure and seek to make it compatible with diversity of central message and with diversity at the periphery. Nevertheless, central's inherently limited informational capacity restricts the scope of adaptation. For central remains in both cases the principal decision point, the filter for information, and the initiator of response to change.

In more radical governmental responses to the failure of the center-periphery model, central no longer formulates and promulgates a central message. Instead, it picks up the policy themes around which peripheral messages develop as variants. Peripheral messages are no longer instances of central policy but variations on central policy themes. Central sets out to help peripheral systems transform themselves and to connect them with each other. It goes 'meta' with respect to these discovered systems, prodding them to develop evaluative processes conducive to learning and linking them in learning networks.

In the 'Movement', nuclei of leadership emerge and shift. The informal networks among members are good enough, the infra-structure powerful enough, the central themes of innovation strong and attractive enough, for the system to hold itself together as a learning system without any central facilitator or supporter of the transformations.

In our society the institutional map consists largely of organizations defined at high levels of specificity, whose growth and diffusion take place in the center-periphery mode. Although the institutional map of a society is always in some degree mismatched with the problems thought worth solving, the loss of the stable state makes this state of mismatch universal and endemic.

In response, learning systems have begun to develop in diverse forms—business systems and constellation firms, new ways of forming and implementing policy in government, and some of the dominant social movements of our time. All these share two major themes: a shift upward in the level of generality at which organizations define themselves, and a shift away from center-periphery to network modes of growth and diffusion.

These tendencies converge on the concept of network. The design, development and management of networks become pivotal to learning systems.

II Networks

A network is a set of elements related to one another through multiple interconnections. The metaphor of the net suggests a special kind of interconnectedness, one dependent on nodes in which several connecting strands meet. There is the suggestion both of each element being connected to every other, and of elements connecting through one another rather than to each other through a center.

Where social, organizational or interpersonal networks are in question, there is the concept of channels of relationship among elements, which make it easier or more likely for transactions of a certain kind to occur among elements than if those channels were not present. There is, then, the notion of flows or processes which occur preferentially within the network. In the first instance, networks can be defined through the nature of their elements (for example, persons, departments, organizations), the nature of the channels connecting them (formal lines of authority, information or decision; interpersonal bonds) and the nature of the transactions that can occur through these channels (in this sense, there may be 'referral', 'early warning', 'distribution', or 'money-lending' networks).

On a secondary level, networks may be characterized by their scope, complexity, stability, homogeneity, and flexibility.

There are the formal networks within established organizations—for example, the networks related to command, information, or distribution of goods within a large firm. And there are the informal or 'underground' networks connecting persons, groups and organizations. These are used to circumvent, supplement or replace the operations of formal organizational systems.

Informal networks have long served to enable people to get things done when the formal networks failed. The Russian 'tolkatch', for example, created through his own person informal relationships of exchange between units of Soviet industry; functioning illegally, he compensated for errors in planning and enabled industrial systems to work which would otherwise have been hopelessly paralyzed. All large organizations—military and governmental bureaucracies are famous for it—have their interpersonal networks for exchanging favors on which much business depends. The very life of social systems has depended on the operation of informal networks.

Ad hoc networks have long since come into being to compensate for mismatches between the institutional map and problems perceived as important. In poor black communities, for example, informal networks of 'nannies' often care for the sick and the young. With the loss of the stable state, *ad hoc* networks become a permanent rather than an interim expedient. They begin to occupy a place in the foreground.

In a variety of ways, such informal networks substitute for institutionalized functional systems.

◆   Consider the function of nutritional care for infants. Within a small and relatively well-defined community, such as one related to a housing project, the nutritional well-being of infants in poor families depends directly on factors such as the mother's nutritional knowledge, her presence in the home and her attitude toward the child, the disposable income available for food, the adequacy of appliances including the size of the refrigerator, the mother's access to retail stores. Less directly, it may depend on the family income, the transpor-

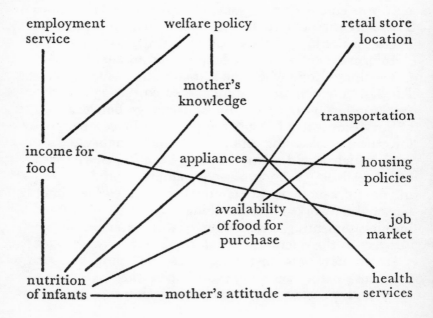

tation available to the family, the location and
pricing policies of retail stores.

This is an obviously incomplete list. It is equally
obvious, however, that all of these factors may be
critical to nutritional care of infants, and that
nearly all fall under the purview of different agencies and individuals. No one controls all of the elements relevant to the nutritional care of infants.
No one agency has both responsibility and authority to carry out that function. Anyone seeking to
carry it out, therefore, must find ways of linking
together or negotiating the separate agencies and
organizations. He must make them aware of the
problem and cause them to harmonize their actions
to solve it (creating a sort of concerted network in
which they participate) or he must negotiate with
each of them and through his own activities cause
them to behave in ways that are conducive to nutritional well-being. In either case, he will have
knitted these separate elements together and will
have produced a 'nutritional care network'.

The example might as well have had to do with health
care, care for the aged, employment—indeed, with any
major social function. In each instance, an attack on the
'whole problem' becomes possible only through an informal network such as the one sketched out above, for
no established agency contains all the elements which
must act together in concert in order to carry out the
function.

Often it appears impractical, or impossible, to leap
from the state in which there is no institution charged
with carrying out a major function to the state in which
an institutionalized functional system exists. The problem of design may be too complex. There may be a need
for probing or testing out before commitment to an institutional design. In such a case, the network created

may serve as a kind of 'shadow system' for the creation of the functional system itself.

◆ Areas on the outskirts of major cities, or in the corridors between them, take on the character of what has been called 'spread city'. They consist primarily of one-family dwellings, spread out at low density, punctuated at rare intervals by commercial and service centers. Poor people, if they inhabit these areas, live at a clear disadvantage because of the inadequacies of public transportation. The grid-work of spread city lends itself to, because it was built around, the technology of the automobile.

Non-drivers—the poor, the old, the very young, and the sick—find themselves cut off from essential services and even from jobs. The cost of transportation to and from work, for example, may exactly cancel out the difference between what they receive from welfare support and the wages they would get when starting a job.

If such an area were to be photographed, at intervals of ten to fifteen years, over long periods of time, it would show a gradual progression from countryside to densely settled metropolitan area. Its current state appears as an intermediate stage. Within this context, planners have projected an extensive mass transit system. But reluctance to make such a capital investment *before* dense population has built up causes the project to be deferred. In addition, no one is clear what the overall path and route structure should be.

Actual approaches to the short-term transportation needs of the area have taken the form of a series of *ad hoc* measures—jitneys, taxis, buses—each designed to connect non-drivers with essential services at minimum time and cost. Some of these measures are supported by county agencies, some by the service agencies themselves. Taken together, these measures constitute a kind of 'action planning' network for transportation. By observing patterns of use, planners can assess real demand for route connections; changes in the *ad hoc* routes can be made to explore what the pattern of use in a modified system might be.

The set of *ad hoc* transportation services constitutes, in effect, a shadow system for a far more costly mass transit system. It is a form of 'action planning'. But it is a form of planning that requires the creation of a transportation, information and planning network out of a series of independent services.

The concept of a 'shadow network', filling the gap between fragmented services and a more highly aggregated functional system, has applications in many fields other than transportation. It is, for example, a not uncommon stage in the reorganization of companies, and in the passage from one governmental administration to another. It is a response both to the need for smoothness of transition and to the uncertainties inherent in the design of larger functional systems.

The need to establish networks as a step towards more highly aggregated functional systems has its parallel in the problems of attempting to reform a fragmented service system. National systems for health, welfare and employment, for example, are systems in which no one controls all the essential elements. And yet the systems have multiple roots. Like the building industry, each has its multiple constituencies and vested interests among providers and other related beneficiaries, and an effort to intervene in the system may be the one act capable of pulling these separate interests together in a solid, resistive body.

◆ Consider the national system of services to children. It includes services related to physical health (prevention, treatment, rehabilitation), social welfare and mental health. It consists of thousands of public and private agencies, spread throughout the country, each at national, regional, State and local levels. Many of these agencies (for example, those relating to day care) connect 'upward' to agencies organized at the national level around particular service functions (for example the Children's Bureau). Each has its professional and occupational associations; its network of laws, administrative regulations and practices; its pressure groups and constituencies.

The system behaves in roughly the same way towards its actual and potential users as does the blindness system in our earlier example. That is, it serves about 20 per cent—and those generally the least needy—of the population at risk. If it were to try to put this right—but while keeping its staff-client ratios and job structures unchanged—it would be constrained first by manpower and only secondly by dollars.

Like the blindness system, the 'children's system' has been able to keep itself relatively intact over long periods of time, in spite of its growing mismatch with the needs of its client population.

In the light of its multiply-rooted dynamic conservatism, what kind of intervention would help the system reform and redirect its activities? It would need, at a minimum, to have an impact on:

Legislators, at State and national levels

Administrators of children's agencies, at several levels

Parents' organizations

Middle-level bureaucrats within children's agencies

Officials of agencies governing regulations affecting children's services

Innovators or entrepreneurs of new services for children

Officials of city and State governments

Key figures in relevant professional associations

Journalists and representatives of the various media whose comments affect children's services.

But these actors and agencies are largely independent of one another, operate in different spheres which 'meet' only around certain particular issues, respond to different kinds of pressures and interests, and live and work in widely dispersed geographical areas. Clearly, any large-scale attempt to intervene in the system would need, at some point, to connect to each of these interests and to connect to them in ways that count. But this could not be done by an individual or a single organization. It would need to take the form of a network of organizations and individuals, chosen for their ability to make contact with essential elements of the children's system. In this sense, the organization put together to influence the children's system would have to be in the nature of a network mirroring many aspects of the system itself.

Network roles

The dominance of networks and network organizations makes a series of new demands on persons. A new set of roles becomes dominant. To the extent that we experience a real impetus in the direction of learning systems, the priorities will be increasingly on what might be called network roles. These roles are essential to the design, creation, negotiation and management of *ad hoc* and continuing networks. They include the following:

◆ *Systems negotiator*   The ombudsman, guide, middle-man or 'tolkatch' who serves as the vehicle by which others negotiate a difficult, isolated, rigid or fragmented system.

◆ *'Underground' manager*   He maintains and operates informal, underground networks. Through personal relationships, he maintains a coherent operation—for example, across governmental agency lines—sometimes pursuing in this way functional goals that have little or nothing to do with the formal policies of the agencies involved.

◆ *Manoeuvrer*   He operates on a 'project' basis, and is able through personal networks to persuade or coerce institutions to make the shifts required to realize a project that cuts across institutional lines. Real estate 'packagers', or the effective managers of a housing or renewal agency in virtually any large city, stand as examples of the type.

◆ *Broker*   In the literal, commercial sense a broker connects buyers and sellers. He helps each to identify the other, serves as a channel for information (in principle, there would be no need for brokers if information flow were perfect) and makes 'deals' if he is able to convince buyer and seller that each has something the other wants.

Often, he also serves to clear away the institutional, regulatory and administrative debris which stands in the way of transactions, performing these functions both because of his superior knowledge of the necessary steps and because of his willingness to cope with this level of detail.

Metaphorically the broker can be the person who functions as 'matchmaker' at all levels and in all sorts of functional domains. He maintains a personal network which cuts across critical elements of the systems to be dealt with. Through it, he is able to connect those seeking particular skills, powers or entrées, with the persons capable of providing them. He makes himself the 'node' connecting various strands which are otherwise disconnected. He establishes his position by protecting his 'contacts', by giving reliable access to resources, by the values he shares with his networks, or by his skills in establishing and maintaining personal relations.

(Marion Wright, at the time a young lawyer for the NAACP, made herself for several years in the Mississippi Delta virtually the sole individual trusted by the many local black groups, sympathetic elements of the white power structure, government agencies, and outsiders anxious to funnel money or help to the cause of civil rights in Mississippi.)

◆ *Network manager* He oversees official networks of activities and elements, assuring the flows of information, the processes of referral, tracking and follow-up, and the provision of resources required for the network to operate.

◆ *Facilitator* He attempts to foster the development and interconnection of regional enterprises, each of which constitutes a variant of central themes of policy or function. His role is at once that of consultant, expediter, guide, and connecter. He must provide, as well, the 'meta' functions of training and consultation which enable regional operators to establish and maintain their own networks.

(This has been the mode of operation of outstanding Foundation executives, such as Paul Ylvesaker, as well as certain managers of federal programs who have learned—frequently counter to official doctrine—to treat themselves as facilitators rather than as monitors or enforcers.)

Network roles such as these vary in character and yet make common demands on their practitioners, each of whom attempts to make of himself a node connecting strands of a network which would otherwise exist as disconnected elements. The risks of the roles are many, since the broker may often be squeezed between the elements he is trying to connect. The need for personal credibility is high, since each role demands that the person be acceptable and believable to different organizations and persons, each of whom tends to hold different criteria for acceptance.

For these reasons, people capable of playing network roles frequently occupy places in several of the subsystems among which they must operate. They sustain many organizational identities, and exist on the margins of institutions. They are, in effect, marginal men, with both the negative connotations (of not being central) and the positive connotations (of being at the forefront) suggested by that term. Often this marginality has its compensation through membership in an extensive interpersonal network which serves both the needs of brokerage and personal security.

At present, no one learns to play network roles through formal education or training, any more than he learns through professional training to handle all of the elements involved in tackling whole problems. The demands of learning systems, and the network roles following from those demands, have their implications for professional education. By shifting the nature of the foreground roles, they shift the priority of demands on the person.

◆ 7 What can we know about
◆ social change?

I have argued that the loss of the stable state intensifies
our need for public learning. If we are to avoid the perpetual disruption that goes with insurgency and invasion
as the sole means of breaking dynamically conservative
systems, then we must learn to develop learning systems.

But the very phenomenon that requires this may also
make it impossible. Contrary to mythology, we are
largely unable to 'know' in situations of social change, if
the criteria of knowledge are those of the rational/
experimental model. The constraints on knowing affect
not only our ability to gain certainty, or probability, or
precise knowledge, but our ability to establish knowledge
in the rational/experimental mode at all.

Whereas the rational/experimental mode of knowledge requires that knowledge derived from experiment
apply to the next comparable instance, the loss of the
stable state means that it won't be the same next time.
And the loss of the stable state attacks the social underpinnings of rational knowledge.

Ideology and power-play both respond non-rationally
to limits on knowledge. But we are not forced to choose
between rational/experimental knowing and no knowledge at all. There is another mode of knowing, with its
own heuristics, available to us in situations of social
change, once we are free of scientism. This sort of knowledge does not relieve us of the anxiety associated with

uncertainty, but depends upon an ethic for social learning.

The rational/experimental model assumes that public action is a form of experiment designed to test the hypotheses of public policy. The testing of policy leads to its modification and to renewed testing. Iterations of this process of inquiry converge on 'right', 'true', or 'appropriate' policy. The model rests on what Raymond M. Hainer has described as pragmatism.

> The method of pragmatism is that of recurrent formulation, deduction, test in reality, detection of difference between expectation and findings, and feeding back of the error into the formulation until the difference between the new expectation and the latest look at reality becomes arbitrarily small. Pragmatism implies successive model building, model testing in reality, and feedback of the error to correct the model until convergence on an accurate representation of reality, but is subject to later change if a 'better' or more precise model is invented or discovered. Revision, in principle, may continue without end.
>
> Pragmatism is presumed to be applicable to any phenomena, subjective or objective, people or things, so long as experiments can be validated—that is, the error function is sensibly convergent or, more generally, not divergent. . . .
>
> Reproducibility, separation from calendar time, and independence of place, of ambient conditions, or of 'unnatural influences', are all important as requirements for useful—and in particular, scientifically useful—pragmatic concepts.[1]

The key notion in this passage is that of convergence on a probable conclusion. The rational/experimental model claims probability, not certainty. It admits, even depends upon, error as an essential feature of its method. But it assumes a line of inquiry convergent on univocal statements whose truth lies precisely in their position at the limit of that convergence.

When the rational/experimental model is applied to public learning, it results in a series of assumptions:

- It is possible to establish, independent of think-so, what is happening in the situation. It is possible to know, within tolerable margins of error, what the circumstances are that require public action.

- It is possible to diagnose those events, to establish reasonable hypotheses about their causes.

- It is possible to test these hypotheses—to collect data from existing situations or to construct experimental situations, which will confirm or deny these hypotheses. Experiment of this sort should meet the usual conditions of experiment. There must be controls which allow us to attribute the phenomena observed to some factors and not to others. The experiment must be independent of calendar time, place and ambient conditions; others should be able to repeat it and arrive at similar conclusions.

- Implicit in this is the assumption that we can evaluate the results of experiment; that is, we can attribute observed results to actions we have taken.

- It is possible to extrapolate from, or generalize, the results of experiment: in short, to derive policy from them. We can identify other situations comparable in crucial respects to the experimental one, so that comparable results will appear in these other situations when we take comparable action. It is further assumed that the comparable features of these situations will hold steady over the period of time required to take action.

- It is possible to generalize from the results of limited public action in the sense of 'scaling up'. It is assumed that the process of scaling up will alter only quantitatively, and not in kind, the nature of the conclusions drawn.

Each of these assumptions deserves examination in its own right.

Knowing what's happening

Returning for a moment to the blindness system, there is no aspect of 'what's happening' more important for public policy than the size and make-up of the blind population. But the quality of available data concerning the blindness system in the United States is incredibly poor. There is both an overwhelming array of information and a scarcity of reliable, unambiguous data pertinent to the central questions of management. No statistic is clear and firm. As a consequence, *no significant quantitative generalizations about the system can now be made with a high degree of precision or probability.*

At the present time, there are three principal and widely varying estimates of the number of blind persons in the United States.

Source	Prevalence rate per 1,000	Total number in USA
MRS Projection to total (1965)	1·5	290,000
NSPB Fact Book (1965)	2·1	416,000
National Health Survey	5·6	1,090,000

The sources of the variation become clear as we examine the different bases on which the estimates were made.

The Model Reporting Areas (MRA) are associated States which maintain registers of persons with severe vision impairment. There are at present fourteen such States. The term 'blindness' as used by the Model Reporting Area includes severe vision impairment and is defined in the following way: 'Visual acuity of 20/2,000, if the widest diameter of the field of vision subtends an angle no greater than 20°.' This is a variant of the standard, administratively accepted definition of 'legal blindness'.

National MRA-based figures were obtained by projecting MRA estimates of average prevalence for its fourteen States to the entire population of the United States, taken as 194,000,000.

Finally, the MRA reporting system requires that persons enter the blindness register through an ophthalmologist who uses the standard Snellen charts as tests. There is evidence that ophthalmologists may under-report blindness in two ways: first, by failing to report as officially blind relatively well-to-do patients who wish to avoid the stigma of blindness; and secondly, by failing to encounter legally blind people who, through poverty or ethnic group, fall outside the medical system in which going to an ophthalmologist would be a normal event.

The Fact Book of the National Society for the Prevention of Blindness, Inc. (NSPB) reaches its estimates by projection according to demographic data from the various States and arbitrary weighting factors tied to the number of people in the blindness register in the State of North Carolina.

The National Health Survey derives its data from household interviews on a sample of the civilian population of the United States not living in institutions. It classifies someone as severely visually impaired if he cannot read ordinary newsprint with glasses; or, for a person under six years of age or one who cannot read, if he is given a report of 'blind in both eyes'.

The National Health Survey relies on interviews and employs no test of visual acuity. But even when the standard Snellen charts are used, serious questions of methodology arise. The Snellen chart lacks fine graduations between 20/100 and 20/200, yet this range is the most critical from the standpoint of classification. That is, because of the lack of graduations, anyone tested at twenty feet whose visual acuity is less than 20/100 gets tested next at 20/200. The Snellen chart does not test near vision, which is a better criterion than the 'distance vision' it measures. It does not measure other components of visual performance such as uniformity of field. Lastly, the Snellen chart, taken by itself, indicates mainly the ability of a subject to read a Snellen chart. It does not indicate whether he has useful travel vision, reading vision, or other visual capabilities.

Thus, estimates of the number of blind vary with the definition of blindness used, the method of testing and the sample from which projections are made. *Of the three estimates, the high is more than three times the low.*

Even so, the data on the numbers of the blind is rather better than that on the effect or cost of services provided for the blind, or the numbers of blind persons receiving benefits from agencies not considered blindness agencies. Some of these data are literally impossible to obtain because of the organization or confidentiality of agency reporting systems.

As a consequence, it is difficult to describe, much less evaluate, the blindness system. A conspiratorial mind might construe this state of affairs as a defense mechanism adopted by the system against unwanted inquiry or change. In fact, there is a rather common sort of dialogue between critics and defenders of the system which is of the following pattern:

Critic: The system is in bad shape.
Defender: I don't believe it.
Critic: Look at the facts.
Defender: Where did you get those numbers? They are incomplete and unsound. I can think of a dozen exceptions to them.
Critic: Then let's get better facts.
Defender: We're interested in people, not numbers.

The effect is much as though the system wished to protect itself from scrutiny.

Without resorting to conspiratorial theory, it is apparent that the effort to establish probable statements about the blind runs aground on vague and conflicting definitions of key terms, incompatibility of methods for gathering elementary data and therefore of the data bases established by the various methods, and a reporting system which introduces its own systematic distortions. It is equally apparent that it would cost a great deal of money to remedy these deficiencies, even if they are in principle remediable. A national blindness survey, combining the best features of the existing surveys, would cost many millions of dollars. An appropriation for this purpose is highly unlikely to be made, at least within the next few years. At least in the short term, inquiry into blindness policy will need to be conducted in the absence of this critical information. The effect is very much as though the data were in principle unknowable.

The situation with respect to blindness is not significantly different from that of other social or medical problems. The data on crime, for example, or the disabilities of children or the numbers of the mentally ill, are similarly divergent, vague and fragmentary. From my own observation of many categories of social problem this state of the data is the norm, rather than the exception. The data reflecting the scope and gravity of the problem depend upon the various reporting systems and frequently say more about those systems than about the problems reported. Thus, Commissioner Leary, by enforcing a more stringent reporting of crimes, is said to have doubled New York City's crime rate in one year. And the State of Kansas, by the simple expedient of confining aged patients to facilities classified as geriatric, increased the turnover rate in its mental hospitals.

There is an additional problem widespread in areas of social policy, which affects not only the quality of data but access to it in the first instance. Data gathering is a political process. In a black center-city community, for example, it is not feasible to gather elementary data—family size and make-up, housing conditions, employ-ment patterns, and the like—without solving the political problems of entry into the neighborhood. And the means of solution will affect the quality of the data. If local inter-viewers are hired and trained, usually through contact with a neighborhood political leader, their ways of perceiving enter into the data. In one survey of solid waste and the 'cleanliness' of neighborhoods, it became apparent that local and outside observers literally saw different things; their reports conflicted because they perceived differently.

In some cases, the political forces may prevent the gathering of any data at all. In the Mississippi Delta, for example, it has been for years impossible to establish an accurate census of local unemployed blacks—accurate, that is, to within hundreds of thousands—because blacks would not be likely to give accurate information to whites, and local white plantation owners will not allow black investigators on their premises. The problems in a situation of this kind turn out to be problems for the gathering of data, as well.

Even where it appears possible to secure the data, the data may not endure. Once a situation has been des-cribed, will it hold steady beneath that description during the time required for public action? There is, for ex-ample, very little data of any kind about patterns of mi-gration within large cities or from rural areas into cities. The decennial census is of little use, for policy decisions dependent on population movements will come up more than once every ten years. In New York City there are patterns of rapid movement of blacks and Puerto Ricans between points in Harlem, East Harlem and the South Bronx. Decisions about housing and services depend on knowing, for example, how many welfare families will be living in the South Bronx over a period of five years. But the 1960 data no longer apply to the situation in 1968 or 1969. The cost of tracing or 'tagging' migrants on a large scale is excessive. Relatively small samples yield an ambiguous picture. The meaning of a patch of data would vary significantly, for example, depending on whether it were taken to be a segment of a curve rising linearly or exponentially.

To take a more dramatic instance, plans for relocation services in an urban renewal area depend upon estimates of the number of families remaining in the area. The interested actors in that situation have reasons for diminishing or inflating the number. The housing authority, for example, will want to see the number as small as possible. But the number of families remaining in the area may shift rapidly in a period of a few months. A survey of 2,000 families taken in December may be inapplicable by the following June, as families flee the area. And their flight may be a consequence of rumor of demolition, which interested parties can spread.

One may object to all of the above that we have not yet distinguished the different criteria for 'good data', depending on the purposes for which data are to be used. There is a great difference, for example, between the nature of the evidence required to support the conclusion that 'some shift in attention must be made in the direction of the aged blind', as against the evidence required to support the conclusion that 'resources should be divided proportionately (plus or minus 10 per cent) among the age groups of the blind'.

Even for the first case, however, all the blindness data permit us to say is that the several otherwise conflicting estimates concur in showing a growing predominance of aged blind. But none of these concurring estimates is much good! At best, then, the conclusion represents a useful *perspective* on the problem of resource allocation—a perspective subject to continuing review while we implement the policies derived from it. For example, do old people materialize in response to new forms of service oriented to them?

In some cases, we may be able to obtain data which indicate what is happening within reasonable limits of precision, reliability and confidence, for certain levels of policy decisions. But there are many situations in which problems of methodology, definitions, and reporting systems simply do not permit us to know essential elements of what is happening; other situations in which political constraints or practical constraints of cost and time make us behave as though this were the case; and still others in which data secured at one time will not hold steady for policy to be enacted at a later time. Even conclusions which appear to be legitimately drawn from the data must be treated as perspectives on the situation rather than as valid and stable conclusions about it.

Diagnosis

The phrase 'what is happening?' is ambiguous. It may refer to the 'data' or to 'the meaning of the data'. Although there is no firm line to be drawn between facts and their interpretation, there is an important functional distinction to be drawn between a given statement of fact and the subsequent interpretation of the meaning of that fact.

There is in any public inquiry a functional ladder of interpretation—a ladder in which each rung is the 'interpretation' of the 'fact' signified by the rung below. The higher one climbs on that ladder, the more one becomes aware of what I shall call the *Rashomon* effect, in which the same story, told from the point of view of several participants, fragments into several different and incompatible stories. What the story of *Rashomon* displays as a curiosity, situations of public action present as a fundamental condition of inquiry.

Characteristically, situations of public action take the form of interlocking systems of 'actors', each involved in a different key role, each with his own interests, his own perspectives, and his own access to information. Not surprisingly, the nature of the public problem appears to different actors in different and often incompatible ways. To accept the perspective of some outside 'change agent' or 'researcher' as a means of resolving that conflict is to yield unacceptably to the *hubris* of the change agent or the *hubris* of the researcher. There is no inherent reason why his perspective should be used to establish the meaning of the situation.

Tolstoy describes in *War and Peace* the real-world situation of the planner or policy-maker.

For people accustomed to think that plans of campaign and battles are made by generals—as any one of us sitting over a map in his study may imagine how he would have arranged things in this or that battle—the questions present themselves: Why did Kutuzov during the retreat not do this or that? Why did he not take a position before reaching Fili? Why did he not retire at once by the Kaluga road, abandoning Moscow? and so on. People accustomed to think in that way forget, or do not know, the inevitable conditions which always limit the activities of any commander-in-chief. The activity of a commander-in-chief does not at all resemble the activity we imagine to ourselves when we sit at ease in our study examining some campaign on the map, with a certain number of troops on this and that side in a certain known locality, and begin our plans from some given moment. A commander-in-chief is never dealing with the *beginning* of any event—the position from which we always contemplate it. The commander-in-chief is always in the midst of a series of shifting events and so he never can at any moment consider the whole import of an event that is occurring. Moment by moment the event is imperceptibly shaping itself, and at every moment of this continuous, uninterrupted shaping of events the commander-in-chief is in the midst of a most complex play of intrigues, worries, contingencies, authorities, projects, counsels, threats and deceptions, and is continually obliged to reply to innumerable questions addressed to him, which constantly conflict with one another.

Learned military authorities quite seriously tell us that

Kutuzov should have moved his army to the Kaluga road long before reaching Fili, and that somebody actually submitted such a proposal to him. But a commander-in-chief, especially at a difficult moment, has always before him not one proposal but dozens simultaneously. And all these proposals, based on strategies and tactics, contradict one another. A commander-in-chief's business, it would seem, is simply to choose one of these projects. But even that he cannot do. Events and time do not wait. For instance, on the 28th it is suggested to him to cross to the Kaluga road, but just then an adjutant gallops up from Miloradovich asking whether he is to engage the French or retire. An order must be given to him at once, that instant. And the order to retreat carries us past the turn to the Kaluga road. And after the adjutant comes the commissary-general asking where the stores are to be taken and the chief of the hospitals asks where the wounded are to go, and a courier from Petersburg brings a letter from the sovereign which does not admit of the possibility of abandoning Moscow, and the commander-in-chief's rival, the man who is undermining him (and there are always not merely one but several such), presents a new project diametrically opposed to that of turning to the Kaluga road, and the commander-in-chief himself needs sleep and refreshment to maintain his energy, and a respectable general who has been overlooked in the distribution of rewards comes to complain, and the inhabitants of the district pray to be defended, and an officer sent to inspect the locality comes in and gives a report quite contrary to what was said by the officer previously sent, and a spy, a prisoner, and a general who has been on reconnaissance, all describe the position of the enemy quite differently. People accustomed to misunderstand or to forget these inevitable conditions of a commander-in-chief's actions describe to us, for instance, the position of the army at Fili and assume that the commander-in-chief could, on the 1st of September, quite freely decide whether to abandon Moscow or defend it; whereas with the Russian army less than four miles from Moscow, no such question existed. . . .[2]

This passage describes the *Rashomon* effect and a great deal more. Tolstoy understands real-life uncertainty. The implementer of public policy, like the commander-in-chief, works in a situation whose inherent ambiguity expresses itself through the incompatible perspectives of the key actors.

The conflict of incompatible perspectives cannot be resolved only by waiting to hear more of what the data say. New data may yield new perspectives, or may aggravate old differences. In one way or another, conflicts of perspective must be resolved through action. The policymaker may seize a horn of the dilemma and commit himself to a course of action, or he may begin to move in the situation, holding back from those actions which would commit him irrevocably to one perspective or another, seeking to learn from the situation in process, listening to what the situation has to teach as he probes it. Or he may try to bring together the representatives of incompatible perspectives and confront them with one another.

These forms of resolution reflect different traits of character and styles of inquiry. They may be more or less desirable depending on the time-frame for action, the urgency of the situation, and the priority placed on building a group or team through the inquiry. But each form of resolution requires some commitment to action in an uncertain situation *before* the formulation of a clear picture of the nature of the problem. Diagnosis comes about through intervention.

Designing the experiment

In the rational/experimental model of public learning, there is a stage at which some limited public action must occur. In most formulations of the model, it is unclear whether this public action is an experiment or a demonstration. In both, there is intervention and observation of the results. But a demonstration aims at 'success' while in a public experiment 'negative results are as good as positive'. In public experiment one attempts to discover what it was in the intervention that produced the results, while in a demonstration we cannot say that some variables are central to success or failure and others not. If we try to structure the demonstration so that this can be done, demonstration verges on experiment.

It is of the essence of experiment, whether in the physical or social sciences, to allow some factors to vary while others remain constant. This may be done by shifting the values of some variables while holding others constant in a single, continuing experimental situation; or by constructing or finding more than one situation comparable in all respects except for the variables of interest.

But in situations of public learning, it is almost never possible to hold some variables constant while manipulating others. Any intervention affects more than one variable; no move has only its intended consequences. And it is never possible to find a 'control' situation comparable to the experimental situation in all respects except the crucial one.

Take the problem of designing an experiment to learn what constraints need to be overcome and what steps need to be taken in order to increase the supply of low income housing. Among the variables at issue are those related to method of financing, Federal program support, character of sponsor group, building type, technology, and method of land acquisition. It is not feasible to hold all values of these variables constant except one which is given first one value and then another in the 'same situation'. For the situation is critically affected by the first action. The second house on a block, or the second project in a neighborhood, is different in non-trivial ways from the first because of the changes radiating out from the first. Nor is it possible to find another situation which will be comparable in all respects other than the one to be tested. The shift from one neighborhood or one city to another carries with it changes which may in themselves be critical to the effectiveness of the project.

These are problems peculiar to experiment. But there are other problems shared by demonstration as well as experiment. These affect the passage from 'the data' and 'the diagnosis' to the design of limited action.

To return to the example of low-income housing, given the relevance of such factors as user groups, technology, building type, financing method, and the nature of the sponsor, among others, how would one go about designing an experiment or demonstration? Two kinds of problems present themselves. The first is that, in most instances of this kind, we do not even know the names of the variables. We do not know what variable characteristics of the factors listed above will contribute significantly to the results of action. The second has to do with the *number* of variables—assuming we know their names. Which particular values of user group, building type, financing method and technology shall we bring together? Is it useful, for example, to combine a 'black, low income' user group with a low-rise garden type of building, using precast concrete, and 221d-3 financing? Given the number of variations which may be relevant, indeed crucial, for each factor, the resulting matrix of combinations is simply too complex to display and evaluate. Efforts at pruning and simplification of variables for purposes of experiment tend to have the usual effects of the Procrustean bed—one ends up talking about a situation that may be manageable but has little intrinsic interest.

The problem has its analogues in any demonstration or experiment relevant to a new public policy. One could find problems of equal complexity in 'medical manpower', 'guaranteed income', 'health services', and the like.[3]

The conclusion is not that demonstrations cannot be designed, but that in the process there must be certain non-rational steps. It is only on a non-rational basis that one can make the leap from the virtually infinite combinations of possible variables to some finite set.

This is reflected in the way teams or groups often go about their inquiry into problems of public policy. There are characteristic stages of inquiry. There is usually, at first, a period of probing or 'rolling in' the data. The effort is to familiarize the members of the team with the problem. In the course of this effort, early simplistic hypotheses about the nature of the problem may be tried and discarded. There is a growing sense of the complexity of the issues. If the team has not been organized from the outset around a single person, there is apt to be a second stage in which members of the team advance 'their' solutions to the problem. Often these ways of resolving the problem of information overload compete with one another and attach in most group situations to what I have earlier called the politics of inquiry. At this point, the politics of the group process are inseparable from the cognitive process. There is no way to resolve the informational complexity on the basis of cognitive, information-processing activities.

Depending on the timing of deadlines for completion of the tasks, there is a third stage in which the pressures for convergence mount and anxieties about completion run high. These anxieties force the team to *some* resolution of the problem of multiple combinations and possibilities. But several alternative kinds of resolution are possible. The team may fragment, for example, around its several competing figures, and may emerge not with one but with several competing solutions. The team may fail altogether to work out the interpersonal and political issues involved in resolution and may come up with no solution at all. Or the team may coalesce around one solution tied to one person or subgroup which emerges as dominant.

In this final stage, resolution of the informational issues may be achieved through power-play and dominance, but need not be. The emergence of a 'great man' (even on a small scale) and the repression of what does not fit his perspectives on the problem, represent only one kind of interpersonal-cognitive resolution. But there must be some form of interpersonal resolution which permits the resolution of the informational problem. These are not separable in process, and leave their mark on the character of the team. Teams or groups come to be formed through such problem-solving processes, and the team- or group-forming process is itself essential to the resolution of the cognitive issues.

Within this non-rational process, the adequacy of resolution will vary with the team's ability to accept and synthesize apparently conflicting information and perspectives; and this, in turn, will depend on the team's ability to tolerate the mounting anxieties stemming from the pressures for closure in the face of more information than it can handle.

If the problem-solving unit is a person rather than a team, there is still a combination of non-rational and cognitive processes which is essential to closure. In many ways, too, the person 'forms' around his resolution of such issues.

In both cases, convergence on a single design depends upon a non-rational process which, in turn, makes possible the later appearance of rationality.

Extending the results of experiment

The rational/experimental model requires that broad conclusions for public policy be drawn from limited public action. Unless we can extend the results of experiment or demonstration to other situations, there is no point to experiment or demonstration.

Extension includes the process by which results of limited action are interpreted and evaluated. It is the process by which we draw the learning from limited public action and apply it to the next comparable situation or to large numbers of comparable situations. The question, 'What have we learned?' breaks into two further questions: 'What happened?' and 'To what extent and in what ways was it successful?'

Here, issues arise which are quite analogous to those involved in getting the data and formulating a diagnosis.

The *Rashomon* effect crops up again, as it always does in situations of information overload where there are multiple actors with varying perspectives and interests. If we consider the problem of assessing 'what happened' in a demonstration school, for example, there are the following kinds of perspectives to be accounted for:

◆ Students in the school who like it

◆ Students in it who are disaffected

◆ Teachers in it who like it or are dissatisfied

◆ Students out of it who try to get in

◆ Students out of it who couldn't care less

◆ Teachers out of it, covering the full spectrum from approval to disapproval

◆ The principal of the high school

◆ The superintendent who's 'baby' it is

◆ Parents—inside and outside, favorably and unfavorably disposed.

Each of these perspectives may be expected to yield a somewhat different picture of what went on. The problem of establishing what happened will be only in part a problem of getting 'more facts', and much more nearly a process of confronting with one another those who hold different perspectives. At this point, such an effort is indistinguishable from the process of intervention itself; and the results achieved will reflect the skills and values inherent in that process.

The *Rashomon* effect applies even more forcefully to the problem of establishing whether or not what happened was successful. Differences over such a judgment reflect differences in criteria for 'success' as well as in perspectives on what occurred. It is not surprising that it is difficult or impossible to find an unambiguously successful social project.

Judgments about the demonstration school may take the following forms, for example:

'Successful because kids and teachers really worked together, had exciting learning experiences.'

'Unsuccessful because of insufficient attention to basic disciplines.'

'Indeterminate until we see how many get into college.'

'Working all right now but the real question is what it will become in a few years' time.'

'Unsuccessful because of negative effects on the *rest* of the system.'

'Successful because of greater freedom, regardless of what else may be said.'

Judgments of this kind reflect differences in underlying theories and values about education, about schools, about young people, and ultimately about life itself. Differences in values at a very fundamental level may well be reflected in differences in judgment about a particular school.

At this point, adherents of a particular version of the rational/experimental model may opt for quantitative measures of success in order to achieve unambiguous judgments based on such measures. But this approach has pernicious effects. The selected measures are always only inferentially related to the criteria of which they are supposed to be measures—'numbers of graduates admitted to college', for example, as a measure of 'excellence of education'. Situations have a way of testing the differences between measures and what they are supposed to measure. On the other hand, when such measures come to be officially adopted, they acquire political force, and lead, as we have seen earlier, to the very nearly universal tendency to 'optimize to the measures'.

The problem of attributing perceived success or failure to one or more factors in the situation raises a new set of problems.[4]

To begin with, why did the first instance work? or if it failed, why did it fail? The identification of *what* it was that succeeded or failed requires a rigorous selection from the informational complexity of what happened. But the practitioner's definition of what he did may bear little relationship to what actually happened. (As John Holt points out, the teacher's tone of voice, that confirms students in knowing when to pay attention, may have more to do with teaching success than does a particular teaching method.) Or the practitioner may not *know* what was important in what he did. Or his definition of what he did may turn him away from observation of something more interesting than he had intended. ('Sensitivity training groups', for example, may achieve personal renewal under the heading of organizational therapy. Self-help housing may turn out to be a way of pulling people out of the poverty cycle, rather than providing better or cheaper housing.)

Often long time-spans intervene between the initial public action and the effort to extract the learning from it. While the action was in process, it may have been possible to gain insights into the connections between certain characteristics of actions taken and of results achieved (though even here, of course, the conditions for insight are different from the conditions for proof). But long after the event, even the conditions for insight tend to be absent.

All of the above applies both to experiment and to demonstration. The distinction between these two forms of limited public action loses its importance the moment we seek to discover what in the demonstration led to its success or failure; for here, again, we encounter the constraints on experimental inference.

In the face of these obstacles we engage in systematic distortions:

◆ There is a tendency to substitute slogans and war-cries for analysis, perhaps in order to generate the energy or the courage for investment in the next instance.

◆ There is an almost universal tendency to repress failures and to amplify successes. Failures go underground, along with the learning that might have been derived from them. The amplification of success goes together with a radical simplification of what went into it, perhaps in order to conform to the requirements of the center-periphery model of implementation of policy.

◆ There is a tendency to treat the project as though it could be generalized to a large family of situations, without identifying the critical differences among potential situations.

◆ There is sometimes a wish to separate the project from the particular persons associated with it. The wish has its roots in the perceived need to extend the project to a large number of instances in a relatively short time, and to do so in the face of a shortage of qualified persons. As a consequence, those who might be able to supply from their own experience a sense of the details underlying the project slogan are absent. The slogan must fly under its own steam. But it may be precisely the people associated with the project who are critical 'variables' in project success.

Or there may be two opposing tendencies at work: the wish to de-personalize the project and the tendency to cast in the role of hero and indispensable Great Man the key person associated with the venture.

Families of programs have characteristic patterns in this respect. There is in some a tendency to dilution and rigidification, as the initial doctrine moves from the hands of the master to progressive generations of disciples. There is an opposing tendency to concentrate energy and resources on those activities which seem most susceptible to extension independent of person—that is, to the most routine, the most easily learned.

◆ There may be, as a result of pressures for performance cited above, a tendency to try to compress the time required for carrying out the project—in particular, the time for selection, preparation and training of all the actors who must play a critical role.

◆ A kind of 'Hawthorne effect' in the first instance (an enhancement of performance due simply to participation in the experiment) may be absent in what follows.

◆ The concern over 'control' may lead to a level of monitoring, evaluation, or enforcement which was absent in the first instance.

All these sources of distortion may be present in one situation or another. There is one major source of uncertainty, however, which is inherent in every process of extension. It stems, again, from the loss of the stable state: the next instance may be critically unlike the experimental one because, during the process of inquiry itself, the situation will have changed in ways one cannot adequately assess in process. The situation of the planner, policy-maker or implementer of policy, is then very much like the situation of Napoleon at the battle of Borodino, as Tolstoy presents it in *War and Peace*.

From the battle-field adjutants he had sent out, and orderlies from his marshals, kept galloping up to Napoleon with reports of the progress of the action, but all these reports were false, both because it was impossible to establish what was happening at any given moment, and because many of the adjutants did not go to the actual place of conflict, but reported what they had heard from others; and also because while an adjutant was riding the couple of versts to Napoleon circumstances changed and the news he brought was already becoming false. Thus an adjutant galloped up from Murat with tidings that Borodino had been occupied and the bridge over the Kolocha was in the hands of the French. The adjutant asked whether Napoleon wished the troops to cross it? Napoleon gave orders that the troops should form up on the farther side and wait. But before that order was given—almost as soon in fact as the sergeant had left Borodino—the bridge had been retaken by the Russians and burnt. . . .

An adjutant galloped up from the fleches with a pale and frightened face and reported to Napoleon that their attack had been repulsed, Campan wounded and Davout killed; yet at the very time the adjutant had been told that the French had been repulsed, the fleches had in fact been recaptured by other French troops, and Davout was alive and only slightly bruised. On the basis of these necessarily untrustworthy reports Napoleon gave his orders, which had either been executed before he gave them, or could not be and were not executed. . . .[5]

A new set of issues arises when the extension of the first instance is not simply to another instance but to a large number of instances. Then, in addition to the constraints on 'extension', we encounter constraints on 'scaling up'.

There is built into the very idea of experiment or demonstration a discrepancy in scale between the first instance and the remaining instances that constitute its extension. This discrepancy can work in several ways. Certain varieties of problem may be insoluble at small scale but manageable at larger scale. This is particularly true with respect to that family of effects grouped under 'economies of scale', but it holds for 'learning curve' effects (improvements in performance over time, due to repetitive practice) and for effects related to 'leverage', as well. For example:

◆ Economies of scale may be essential to success where low cost is a major criterion of success, as in housing rehabilitation.

◆ The 'learning curve' may mean that costs will not reach tolerable levels short of large production runs.

◆ The leverage provided by large-scale aggregation of markets may be essential to control of dissident forces.

On the other hand, features of the project which were effective at small scale may become ineffective at large scale. Or small defects may become amplified. For example:

◆ Workers may lose the ability to provide careful attention to detail as handicraft operation gives way to mass production.

Or certain constraints, absent in the first instance, may be encountered at large scale:

◆ You run out of the 'best places to try it'.

◆ You run out of resources.

◆ You exceed the level of activity that your existing supply of manpower or management can handle.

For all of these reasons, there is considerable likelihood that the conditions of performance at large scale will be different from conditions of performance in the first instance. These differences may be guessed from consideration of analogous processes of scaling up, but they can not be inferred in a particular case from consideration of the first instance alone.

In the face of such inherent uncertainties in learning from experiment or demonstration, and in extension of learning to the next instance or to large scale, how do such judgments in fact get made?

These judgments are conditioned by a variety of social, organizational and political processes—processes which must, according to the rational/experimental model of public inquiry, appear non-rational.

◆ In the case of the early Head Start experience, only a few early investigations had been undertaken, largely in New York, prior to the large scale commitment to the program finally made by the Office of Economic Opportunity.

But those instances looked promising. The idea appealed to Sargent Shriver. There were substantial funds—approximately $90,000,000—still uncommitted. There was a need, as Shriver saw it, to make a dramatic showing. And so the decision was made to leap from one or two instances to a massive program embodying fifty or more projects.

There had been little if any attempt to establish controls for what was done. There had been insufficient experience to separate out perceived effects of the first projects from the influence of the particular persons who conducted them. Certainly there was no opportunity to assess long-term effects.

But on the basis of Shriver's intuitive response, the availability of the resources, the need to make 'a showing', *and the fact that he had the power to make that decision*, the leap was made to the large scale program.

We should note that, for all the subsequent controversy over Head Start, it is by common consent one of the major candidates for significant educational innovation in the last decade. The leap from a few instances to a large number gave the program high visibility and momentum and, while it subjected it to great risk in the long run, made it less vulnerable in the short term to the various dangers and doubts that plague all new programs. A large enough commitment had been made by the agency —in fact, by the administration—so that in the short term the program had to be defended by all those whose interests lay with the agency.

Given the vulnerability of *all* incipient efforts to extend new projects, it may well be that only such a leap to a sizeable commitment will insure that the program survives to the point when its performance at large scale can be assessed.

What is the function of 'first instances' in these cases of non-rational resolution of the questions posed by them?

Their function is in the broadest sense political. They are means by which the ideas of the project may be brought into good currency, by which visibility can be gained, constituencies built, and support gathered for a larger commitment to policy.

There is in effect here a kind of innovation game. Any new social program or policy will encounter the dynamic conservatisms of the social systems built around the technologies and institutions it is likely to displace. There is, moreover, a disinclination to make a large-scale commitment to any program which is untried; such a commitment would be 'irrational'. In this sense, the rational myth of public action supports the dynamic conservatism of established institutions.

But the supporters of the new program must attempt to use the rational myth to their own advantage. They must obtain commitment to a first instance—under the heading of experiment, pilot or demonstration—and they must try, under that heading, to bring the idea of the project into good currency. They must establish its visibility. They must demonstrate its connection, directly or indirectly, with the interests of those who will be powerful in decisions concerning the program. They must build a constituency around it. And they must seek to establish a continuing cumulative commitment that will culminate, if it is successful, in an ideology of support.

In all of this, they must operate within the framework of the experimental myth of public inquiry. They must play the game-within-a-game of inquiry, experiment, evidence, and confirmation.

Into the vacuum created by our inability to provide rational answers to the central questions involved in the extension of first instances—by the accepted standards of the rational/experimental model—there moves a non-rational array of determinants. The process of judgment shifts to the domain of power, prestige, and the resolution of conflicting interests. It becomes, in short, a political process. Inquiry then becomes after-the-fact justification for political positions.

Other ways of knowing

We have considered each step in the rational/experimental model of public inquiry, and have argued, in each case, that the kinds of inferences required by the model are not feasible. Although the constraints on the model's application take somewhat different forms for each step, there are certain constants. The situation—whether it is the initial one, or the situation following experiment, or the situation involved in establishing the comparability of the next instance—characteristically displays more information than can be handled. The symptom of this information overload is the *Rashomon* effect, in which different actors generate different and incompatible perspectives on the situation.

Perhaps most important, conclusions will not hold steady over time. The times required for diagnosis, for design of demonstration, or for extension to the next instance, are long enough—in a period of loss of the stable state—to include changes which invalidate conclusions once they are reached.[6]

We have also touched on variants of actual response to the failure of the rational/experimental model. (For this failure is recognized in practice, if not in public utterance.) There are two major forms of response which may, but need not, accompany one another. The first is resolution through dominance. It consists in the substitution of power-play for inquiry. It makes the political dimension of inquiry the exclusive one and treats inquiry itself as a cover or rationale for the resolutions achieved through dominance.

The second is resolution by appeal to ideology, that is, to closed theory or what Eric Hoffer has called 'true belief'. The ideology may be the ideology of the revolutionary, of the reactionary, of the 'liberal', or of the pragmatic technocrat. Its content is less important than the manner in which it is held: namely, theory held as right, inherently and once-and-for-all.

Ideology frequently has a moralistic dimension. A complex action in a complex situation may be condemned in its entirety because it is perceived to involve a component of 'dishonesty', 'pay off', 'racism', 'revolution', 'disregard of authority', or the like. While ideologies differ enormously, they all help their adherents to handle complex situations simply.

It is easy to see how the two modes of resolution may complement one another. Ideology may demand power-play for its imposition on non-adherents. Power-plays require a content around which to exercise power, and that content—if it is imposed rather than inquired into—becomes ideology.

Both may carry with them a version of 'epistemological nihilism' in public affairs—that is, a view that nothing can be known, or that one opinion is as good as another, or that matters of public action must be decided on grounds that have nothing to do with inquiry. I have suggested in the preceding pages that scientism in public policy—adherence to the rational/experimental model of public learning—leads to epistemological nihilism. It causes us to put all our eggs in one basket, and the basket turns out to be unable to hold anything. If scientific knowledge is the only valid kind, and we turn out to be unable to achieve it in public matters, where are we?

Beyond resolution through dominance, or through ideology, and beyond epistemological nihilism, there seem to me to be two major responses to the inapplicability of the rational/experimental model: systems analysis and existentialism.

Both begin with the recognition that situations of public learning present us with more information than we can handle because they display multiple, complex interactions of variables to which no relatively simple, highly predictive theory is adequate.

Both begin with a certain view of the dynamics of patterns of change in social systems. In effect, this view recognizes that phenomena may change over time, in limited contexts, in predictable ways.

In this figure, the curve behaves in predictable ways, describable by a function. But there are also zones in which the behavior of the curve is unpredictable and unstable, as in the figure overleaf.

This zone of instability may be followed by a further zone of stability—but may not; and, at any given point, the duration of the zone of instability is unclear. Both systems analysis and existentialism recognize the zones of instability in which public inquiry takes place.

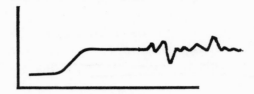

Systems analysis—by which I mean to indicate no particular theory or school, but the overall intellectual tendency of which particular theories and schools are components—seeks to develop ever more adequate models of the interconnected forces, vectors and flows of which changing social situations are composed. Its aim is not the development of a particular theory of a particular social problem. It seeks the development of a more general and powerful set of tools which would make possible the simulation of presently uncertain social situations, converting zones of instability and uncertainty to predictable variations of complex simulations.

Scarcely anyone claims that systems analysis is now able to solve a problem of public policy. But many give their allegiance to a long-term strategy of perfecting, through successive approximations, a tool that will eventually be capable of simulating social situations in all their complexity.

Existentialism, in the rather special sense in which I use it here, derives from the writings of Raymond Hainer.

Existentialism begins with experience, phenomena and existence as these are perceived. Concepts arise out of the uniquely human process of perceiving, of pattern (Gestalt) forming, of symbolizing, of comparing, and of conceptualizing, which are not explicitly conscious. . . . consistency can be assured only through repetition of experience, and consistency is possible only if there is little 'noise' or random uncertainty in the raw data supplied by the senses, if symbols can be used, and if anxieties are within bounds. . . . Descriptions . . . are all that can be drawn from experience; experience of itself is nonverbal, incommunicable, autistic. Descriptions are a simplified version of experience. . . .

In existentialism assumptions cannot be stated. Implications can be discovered, but a finite listing of the implications of existence is not necessarily possible. . . . Temporal prediction is not possible, and anyone predicting the future with certainty is engaged in misrepresentation. . . .

The 'past' and the 'future' are not necessarily meaningful terms; only the 'here-and-now' has meaning; that is, initially only the 'ever-present present' exists and has meaning.[7]

In existentialism, it is taken as given that situations of public action contain more information than we can handle and are inherently unstable. Within them, then, knowledge can have only the validity it is found to have in the here-and-now. The here-and-now provides the test, the source and the limit of knowledge. No theory drawn from past experience may be taken as literally applicable to *this* situation, nor will a theory based on the experience of this situation prove literally applicable to the next situation. But theories drawn from other situations may provide perspectives or 'projective models' for this situation, which help to shape it and permit action within it. However, this process of existential theory-building must grow out of the experience of the here-and-now of this situation, must be nourished by and tested against it. It cannot be the basis for a 'general theory', drawn from this situation, which will prove literally applicable to 'other situations like this'. It will need to be tested against the experience of the next situation, and the next situation may well turn out to be different. We cannot, therefore, speak validly of its 'probability value', or of its 'probable application' to the next instance.

Putting aside the ultimate ambitions of systems analysis, existential knowledge is the kind of knowledge actually available to us in situations of public learning. It is not a new kind of knowledge, but is in fact the characteristic mode of knowing for those whose work is in the domain of public learning. Because of the dominance of the rational/experimental model of knowing, the explicit theory of existential knowledge may appear to be new.

Existential knowledge lends itself to a heuristic—that is, to consideration of the sorts of practices that are conducive to it. And, because it moves from and does not disregard the inherent uncertainty of experience in public learning, it demands an ethic.

The generation and testing of knowing in the here-and-now is central to all forms of existential knowledge.

There is an emphasis on the case history, the narrative, and on what Robert Weiss has called the 'dramaturgic' approach.

Where we cannot establish controls we form judgments most effectively about 'what has happened' or 'what led to these effects' by noting processes *internal* to the project.

◆   The teacher at an experimental school sees how students move from attitudes of distrust and disinterest through periods of 'testing the system' to a growing commitment to the venture as a whole. He receives a thousand little indications that the new climate of commitment and excitement over learning grows out of that developing trust and out of the students' growing sense that they are indeed responsible with the teachers for what will happen.

◆   The consultant to the board of a neighborhood corporation sees unfolding the gradual testing of him and the gradual development of confidence on the part of the group as it begins to be able to do things—to speak to mayors and agency heads, for example—which it had not previously envisaged.

In instances like these, it is possible to *watch* one thing grow out of another. It is possible, occasionally, to observe how actions have precipitated a new state of the system. These 'internal judgments' have severe limitations. The learning agent—the teacher or the consultant, for example—cannot say with confidence that the observed changes would not have occurred under other conditions. He can only guess, and often very tentatively, at what might have happened had he, or someone else, behaved differently. This fact does not of itself invalidate his judgment that, in these circumstances, his action did indeed precipitate this effect.

He cannot assert with confidence that in 'comparable circumstances' others who behaved similarly would achieve comparable effects. It is difficult for him to separate the sequence of events he observed, always under values which enabled him to make sense of complex events, from the specific histories attached to *this* social system and to his person as related to it. But as he moves from situation to situation, he develops more or less explicit 'models' of situation-action-and-effect. These become the bases of personal style and projective models. These are 'models' in the sense of being conceptual pictures of descriptions which relate characteristics of action, situation and outcome at some level of generality. They are 'projective' in the sense of being projected on to the next situation, always as a perspective on that situation and always subject to transformation through contact with that situation.

The extension of these projective models is always problematic. There is always more about the situation in which the learning agent acted and more about the nature and context of his action than he can take account of. It is always to some degree indeterminate whether the next instance will be like the first in the respects that are crucial.

He may be more or less articulate about these models

of action. Others, observing him in context and from the outside, may be more successful than he in making explicit the models under which he operates. Or he may be able, after the fact, to be more articulate than he was in process.

His explicit formulations are always inadequate to his grasp of action and response; that is, he is always somewhat in the position of observing his own responses to situations in order to determine what his principles of action are. And he is always subject to surprise.

Case histories, evolving as projective models, make up, as it were, the store of experience available to the inquirer. As these multiply and function repetitively in the inquirer's experience, he may be led to develop *typologies*. These may be sets of generalized case histories which display patterns of relationship between characteristics of action, situation and outcome. Or they may be simpler distinctions between types of person, types of situation, types of action, with suggestions of relationships to other elements of projective models. Tolstoy's distinction between hedgehog and fox, Rostow's stages of economic growth, Erikson's stages of development of the self—each of these may be regarded as a typology, in the sense intended here. Their significance is not that they divide a certain reality into classes (in the manner of biological classes in natural science) but that, in the absence of a coherent and encompassing theory, they provide ways of organizing items of experience and relating them to new situations. Like the projective models of which they are composed, they are subject in every here-and-now to modification or even to explosion through surprise.

Knowledge of this kind depends upon a variety of conditions.

There must be a knowing and learning agent who maintains continuity over the learning process. He must span the period which includes both the experiences underlying his projective models and the 'next instances' to which those models are brought. That agent need not be an individual. It may be a group or organization which maintains the array of projective models in its social memory and succeeds in doing so even though individuals move discontinuously through the system. But without the continuity of the learning agent, the progressive formation, trial and evolution of projective models cannot occur.

All situations are inherently open-ended, in the sense that before the fact they are susceptible to different projective models. And all projective models are inherently open-ended in the sense that they are susceptible to modification, explosion or abandonment in the face of the next here-and-now.

This open-endedness is incompatible with traditional notions of expertise, or of professionalism—since both these notions carry with them the concept of cumulative bodies of theory which can be applied predictably to situations of a certain kind. In existential terms, 'expertise' and 'professionalism' ride lightly as bodies of theory purporting to explain and guide practice, theories whose relevance is constantly subject to the test of the here-and-now. The loss of the stable state demands the invention of new professions. New bodies of projective models are required, or the revitalization of old ones by their translation across professional and disciplinary lines.

The learning agent must be willing and able to make the leaps required in existential knowledge. These are the leaps from informational overload to the first formulation of the problem, from an absence of theory to convergence on a design for public action, and from the experience of one situation to its use as a projective model in the next instance. These are leaps, because they cannot be justified except by what happens after they are made. They are conditions, not consequences, of knowledge.

The learning agent must be able to synthesize theory, to formulate new projective models, out of his experience of the situation, while he is in the situation. He cannot operate in an 'after-the-fact' mode, taking as given or as *a priori* applicable, theory which is already formulated. And as often as not, his projective models come apart. He must be willing for them to come apart, and to synthesize new theory in process as the old explodes or decays.

In carrying projective models to the next instance, the learning agent must be able to maintain his projective model as a basis for action while at the same time regarding it as a point of view on the situation. If he is unable to act on it, he will be unable to act at all. If he is unable still to regard it as a point of view, he will be incapable of abandoning or modifying it in the here-and-now of the new situation. This paradoxical combination of tentativeness and resolution is the characteristic mode of existence of the projective model; and the ability to sustain it is the characteristic property of the agent of existential knowledge.

The learning agent in situations of public action must be able to confront multiple, conflicting perspectives on the situation with one another. He must be able to sustain and work in the 'interpersonal here-and-now' which is characteristic of public action. The resolution of *Rashomon*-like relativism has only the validity that it is *found* to have in some interpersonal here-and-now.

The learning agent must be willing and able to use himself as an informational instrument within the learning situation. His own abilities to listen rather than assert, to confront and tolerate the anxieties of confrontation, to suspend commitment until the last possible moment—all condition his ability to draw information from the situation while it is in process.

The 'musts' in all of these statements reflect what is in fact an ethic for existential knowing.

These imperatives constitute a code for public learning, but a code that is 'meta' with respect to public learning. It does not in any way specify the content of knowledge, only the conditions of the response and the stance of the person. These conditions may be expressed in the requirement that we seek to resolve certain apparent antinomies:

- The demand for security in situations of uncertainty and anguish which threaten the security of the self

- The demand for conviction, and with it the requirement that beliefs and values be recognized as ways of looking at the world

- Engagement with others, with ultimate reliance on the self recognized as the internalization of others

- The priority of process over product, but with acceptance of such products as survive the test of the here-and-now

- Rejection of the literal past, and acceptance of the past as projective model for present situations.

It is the function of such an ethic both to reflect and to build the strength of the self in its confrontation with the uncertainties inherent in public learning.

❖ Notes

◆ Notes

1 The loss of the stable state

1 This paper is an attempt to develop ideas originally worked out with the late Dr Raymond M. Hainer.

2 I use the word 'pragmatism' here to mean that theory of knowledge or inquiry which assumes the possibility of generating empirically based knowledge of the world, gained through a process that includes:

- the gathering of data
- the generation of hypotheses to explain these data
- the formulation and conduct of experiments to test these hypotheses
- reformulation of hypotheses on the basis of experimental evidence.

The assumption underlying pragmatism, in this sense, is that iterations of the process converge toward knowledge of reality.

A 'particular pragmatism' is a particular complex of data, hypotheses and experiments.

The use is derived from Raymond Hainer's 'Rationalism, Pragmatism and Existentialism', in *The Research Society* Evelyn Glatt and Maynard W. Shelly, eds. Gordon & Breach Inc., 1968, as is much else in this chapter.

3 It is most severe in what Ronald Laing has called 'ontological uncertainty'.

> The individual in the ordinary circumstances of living may feel more unreal than real; in a literal sense, more dead than alive; precariously differentiated from the rest of the world, so that his identity and autonomy are always in question. He may lack the experience of his own temporal continuity. He may not possess an

overriding sense of personal consistency or cohesiveness. He may feel more insubstantial than substantial, and unable to assume that the stuff he is made of is genuine, good, valuable. And he may feel his self as partially divorced from his body.

> R. D. *Laing, The Divided Self* Tavistock Publications, 1960.

4 The characteristics of the socio-technical process peculiar to our time have encouraged the creation of a special sort of scepticism. When we are forced to confront institutions, structures and values radically different from our own; when we are forced repeatedly to make radical transitions in our own lives —we are led to doubt the special status or stability of our present solutions. Some, noticing this scepticism, have attributed it to our increasing historical self-consciousness. But we can easily attribute it to the pervasive, frequent and implosive character of socio-technical change in our society.

> In this historically self-conscious age, few men can ever forget that what seems unquestionably true to one age or civilization differs from what seems unquestionably true to others. And from historical self-consciousness there is but one step—albeit a long and fateful one—to a wholesale historical scepticism; to the despairing view that history discloses a variety of conflicting *Weltanschauungen,* with no criterion for choice between them anywhere in sight.
>
> Emil Fackenheim *Metaphysics and Historicity*
> Marquette University Press, 1961, p. 3.

5 Derek De Solla Price *Big Science, Little Science* Columbia University Press, 1963, pp. 14–15.

6 The subject of scientific and technological discontinuities has been treated at length by Thomas Kuhn in *The Structure of Scientific Revolutions* University of Chicago Press, 1962; by Marshall McLuhan in several of his books; and by Bernard Muller-Thym in his unpublished lectures on 'The End of the Neolithic Age'.

7 Eric Hoffer points out:

> In reality the boundary line between radical and reactionary is not always distinct. The reactionary manifests radicalism when he comes to recreate his ideal past. His image of the past is based less on what it actually was than on what he wants the future to be. He innovates more than he reconstructs. A somewhat similar shift occurs in the case of the radical when he goes about building

his new world. He feels the need for practical guidance, and since he has rejected and destroyed the present he is compelled to link the new world with some point in the past . . .

                Eric Hoffer *The True Believer* Harper & Row, 1951.

This is not the only form of revolutionary response. Paul Goodman's concept of revolution is of a different kind:

Modern times have been characterized by fundamental changes occurring with unusual rapidity. These have shattered tradition but often have not succeeded in creating a new whole community. We have no recourse to going back, there is nothing to go back to. *If we are to have a stable and whole community, we must painfully perfect the revolutionary modern tradition we have.*

                Paul Goodman *Growing Up Absurd*
Random House (New York), Victor Gollancz (London), 1961.

Goodman has a remarkably clear picture of the state toward which revolt should move. It is not total rejection of the past but a perfecting of the best traditions of the past. His vision is in many ways an eighteenth century vision of freedom, order, peace, individuality and creativity. It is revolt with a program and return without reaction. But even Goodman does not confront the implications of the threat to the stability of the ideal condition he depicts as the objective of revolution.

Goodman at times says that the young require belief in a future stable state ('the ideal toward which I am growing') but that adults must 'learn to confront an uninvented and undiscovered present'.

8 Emil Fackenheim outlines, in the work cited earlier, three responses to 'historical scepticism' which make an interesting counterpoint to the anti-responses I have described:

The first (of three contemporary attitudes) is what may be called *sceptical paralysis.* Here historical self-consciousness has led to two results: to the insight that wherever there has been a great purpose there has been a great faith; and to the loss of capacity for commitment to such a faith. Hence there is paralysis which recognizes itself as paralysis and preaches doom.
Then there is what may be called *pragmatic make-believe.* Here . . . [man] falls to pretending to believe hoping that a pretended might do the work of an actual faith. But it cannot . . .
When men truly suffer from this contradiction they may seek

escape in the most ominous form of modern spiritual life: *ideological fanaticism*. . . . ideology asserts itself absolutely . . . it knows itself to be not truth but merely one specific product of history. . . . Hence unlike faith, ideology must by its very nature become fanatical . . . ideology can achieve certainty only by *making* itself true.

2   Dynamic conservatism

1 Elting Morison *Men, Machines and Modern Times* M.I.T. Press, 1966.

2 These tendencies toward increasing disorder may be described as 'organizational entropy', the tendency of social systems to move toward states of greatest diffusion of energy. Organizational entropy manifests itself in a variety of symptoms:

- the dissociation of elements of the organization
- confusion and overlap of function
- 'leakage' through organizational boundaries into adjacent systems
- decline in the level of energy
- 'organizational drift' in relation to clear and steady objectives
- failure to keep internal conflicts within bounds that permit organizational integrity
- descent toward the least demanding and the most routine tasks.

3 Walter Cannon *The Wisdom of the Body* W. W. Norton & Co., 1963, p. 299.

4 W. V. O. Quine *Methods of Logic* Henry Holt & Co., 1960, p. xiii.

5 The dynamism works not only in the domain of research but in the related area of standards. An issue of considerable liveliness in the Department of Commerce, for example, was whether standards for bathtubs should cover resistance to cigarette burns. The issue appeared trivial until it became apparent that this specification would have ruled out fiberglass-reinforced polyester, the major competitor to the traditional porcelain enamel bathtub. A lobby for the cigarette-burn-

resistance requirement had emerged which included, not surprisingly, the makers of porcelain enamel tubs, the related unions, the steel-makers and their associations. The conflict engaged vested interests in the old and the new technologies; and the representatives of the old were at the time stronger, more entrenched, and more effective in working their will through government.

A similar issue, but of far greater magnitude, concerned lumber standards. The literal '2 by 4' had long been out of date. The question now was whether boards marked '2 by 4' should have a thickness of $1\frac{1}{2}$ inches measured at a fixed moisture content, or whether the thickness should be $1\frac{5}{8}$ inches without specification of moisture content.

This seemed one of the less passionate issues of the day, but it ended up by generating approximately 30,000 letters per year—more than any other issue in the recent history of the Department of Commerce. It divided the country into 'wets' and 'drys'. The drys were those few lumber manufacturers large enough to afford a kiln, so that they could make kiln-dried lumber to dimension. And the wets were those tens of thousands of lumber manufacturers too small to afford kiln-drying equipment; because they could not afford it, they would not have been able to meet the new standard.

The standard would, in all likelihood, have eliminated thousands of small producers. It would have shifted the regional balance of lumber production; and it would, it was rumored, have added approximately $500 million dollars to the value of Weyerhauser's timber holdings, simply by enabling that firm to make a greater number of '2 by 4s' from a single tree.

The battle over lumber standards drew in all components of the building industry, a full range of Federal agencies, State governments from Maine to North Carolina, and Congressional representatives to boot; Magnuson and Jackson from Washington, not surprisingly, represented the large 'dry' manufacturers; James Roosevelt, at the time a representative from Southern California, took up the cause of the many small lumber manufacturers in that region. Speeches were delivered on the floor of the House. Many closed door sessions were held. Accusations of illegitimate influence were bandied about. And the entire issue took up more of the time of officials in the

Department of Commerce than I have any means of computing. The intensity of the struggle grew out of the fact that the dynamic conservatism of the industry was threatened, not by a fragile outside force, but by a considerable internal one.

6 Each of these programs represented, at the time of its inception, a significant innovation in what was considered humane treatment for the blind. Each tended, upon acceptance, to become established and frozen in place—aspects of the way services to the blind must operate. The present system represents an array of agencies and service activities dating from different historical periods, based on different assumptions, goals and technologies. The effect is rather like complex geological strata in which entities of widely varying origin and character exist side by side.

7 See the study conducted by the Bureau of Labor Statistics for the American Foundation for the Blind, 'National Survey of Personnel Standards and Personnel Practices and Services for the Blind—1955.'

8 See the BLS study cited above; Robert Scott *The Making of Blind Men* The Russell Sage Foundation, 1969; Eric Josephson *The Social Life of Blind People* The American Foundation for the Blind, 1968; and the OSTI report to the National Institute of Neurological Diseases and Blindness, 'Blindness and Services to the Blind in the United States' 1968. These studies provide the basis for the assertions made in this section.

9 D'Arcy Thompson *On Growth and Form* Cambridge University Press, 1961, p. 11.

10 And so we have industrial departments of 'research', which do produce improvement and technical service. We have programs of 'communication', which disseminate the same old documents. We have departments of 'planning', that perform bookkeeping functions for the same old data.

11 Elting Morison *Men, Machines and Modern Times* p. 36.

12 Bronislaw Malinowski *The Dynamics of Culture Change* Yale University Press, 1945, p. 1.

13 W. W. Rostow *The Stages of Economic Growth* Cambridge University Press, 1960, p. 12.

14 Che Guevara *Guerilla Warfare* Monthly Review Press, 1961.

4 Diffusion of innovation

1 Everett Rogers *Diffusion of Innovations* The Macmillan Co., 1962, pp. 13–14.

2 In fact, later evolutionary developments in diffusion systems do not necessarily eliminate earlier forms; the simple center-periphery model still functions in education and business. And the proliferation of centers, which flowered in the nineteenth century, had its precursors in early history.

3 Rogers op. cit., p. 14.

4 Arthur W. Brayley *History of the Granite Industry of New England* Volume I, published by the Authority of the National Association of Granite Industries of the United States, Boston, 1913, p. 78.

5 ibid., p. 10.

6 ibid., pp. 15–16.

7 ibid., pp. 17–18.

8 ibid., p. 18.

9 ibid., pp. 18–19.

10 Melvin T. Copeland and Elliott C. Rogers *The Saga of Cape Ann* The Bond Wheelwright Company, Freeport, Maine, 1960, p. 141.

11 ibid., p. 147.

12 ibid., pp. 124–5.

13 ibid., p. 147.

14 ibid., pp. 147–8.

15 ibid., p. 142.

16 ibid., pp. 150–1.

17 The whole matter is complicated somewhat by the fact that the reaction of a system to an innovation depends on the ways in which the innovation is perceived by those within the system. The threat inherent in a significant innovation may or may not be apparent at the outset. Where it is apparent, the system is likely to respond by ignoring or by actively resisting the innovation. But where the threat is not apparent, the system may accept the innovation fairly readily as a kind of Trojan horse,

only to experience far-reaching and unanticipated disruption as a consequence. Such appears to have been the case in the well known story of the adoption of the steel axe by Yir Yoront: acceptance of the attractive and apparently innocuous implement led to a chain reaction of cultural disruption. Consumer acceptance of television in our own society may turn out to have been a similar phenomenon.

Or again, the system may be structured in such a way that only a certain element of it, and a relatively powerless one, experiences disruption as a consequence of acceptance. The acceptance of mechanical equipment, chemical fertilizer and weed-killer by cotton planters in the Mississippi Delta turned out to transform the Delta cotton system and in the process to dislocate thousands of black plantation workers. But these were unable to make their resistance felt.

So that our earlier conclusion must be somewhat modified. The diffusion of a significant innovation behaves like our model rather than the Rogers model where the innovation creates a perceptible threat of disruption to elements of the system powerful enough to oppose it.

5   Government as a learning system

1 Implicit in this second requirement for learning is a negative judgment about the feasibility of long-term forecasting. Attentiveness to change in the nature of the problems confronting our institutions can express itself either in a desire to predict future problems in order to design policies and institutions for them ahead of time, or in attempts to make our institutions increasingly flexible and responsive to the changing requirements we are unable to anticipate. Development of the capability for quick, flexible response is a substitute for the ability to predict accurately what lies ahead.

2 The critique of the model, taken as a theory of knowledge, will appear in a subsequent chapter.

3 In a broader sense, there are ideas in good currency in every social system, whether it has a formal public policy or not. In this broader sense, the ideas in good currency, taken together,

make up (in the sense outlined in Chapter 2) the prevailing theory powerful for behavior in the system.

4 There is a precisely opposite pathology to the emergence of ideas in good currency, which consists in a precipitate abandonment of issues, not because they have been resolved or perceived to be inappropriate, but because—for the variety of political and media-related actors involved—the times require a new issue. Failure to resolve the old issue may underlie the abandonment, or signs of public disinterest. For there is an aspect of the life of ideas in good currency which has to do with the limits of the public attention span, or a phenomenon of public fatigue in relation to an issue.

In a recent article in the *Boston Globe*, Robert L. Levey described this pathology.

How short is the life span of an issue?
How issues slide in and out of fashion. This was the Winter of ecological concern. You were something of a square if you weren't ready to admit that your nightmares are filled with gross images of mankind being snuffed by its own smoke.

'I don't see how we can make it to the year 2000,' became the sentence of the season, closely beating out the statement, 'Man is going to have to learn to respect his environment or he will destroy himself.'

Politicians thrilled to these developments. Nothing since the adoration of Mom has been so safe an issue. The liberals, radicals, conservatives and yahoos finally found a boat they could all happily float in. And how the talk escalated . . . end the overheating of water by atomic plants, abolish the gas engine, eliminate the tin can, save the cougar, filter the chimneys, jail the flagrant industrialists, stop cutting the trees and filling the marshes.

And every few weeks something fortuitous, like an oil slick, would occur to keep the outrage at a sufficient level—an outrage that has succeeded in producing virtually no action against the problems except for proposals on various governmental levels that give abusers a few years to think about their misdeeds and come up with a promise that they will stop being bad boys.

Of course a society's capacity to maintain its concern is limited. Like an infant, a society has a short attention span and a low frustration threshold. It must constantly be diverted by new miseries and amusements. As the grave pollution problem undulated through the months, keeping well ahead of last Fall's fashionable issues of nudity and Biafra, a new chord was struck—women's liberation.

You could have read all about women's liberation last year in a variety of truly contemporary publications that weren't so pompous and conservative in their judgment of what is timely as the big magazines and newspapers, but it took until now for the likes of *Life*, *Newsweek* and the *Atlantic* to get around to it and establish it as the big Spring thing.

You remember some of the important ones from last Summer and Spring, don't you? That was when black student militants were shown holding guns. And, oh yes, that was when Caesar Chavez finally got onto the covers. The grape boycott was big, very big. If you had a green table grape in your house, you could lose a lifelong friend over it. Everybody was very worried about the poor Mexican-Americans who were getting it good from the Californian growers. You just had to have sympathy. After all, it was important; it was on the cover.

In case you haven't read about it lately, the grape boycott is still going on. The mimeograph machines are still rolling in tiny under-manned, under-supported offices in all the big cities trying to keep the pressure on the supermarket chains to keep California grapes out. Some Chilean grapes are being sold now and the boycott people contend that lots of California grapes are being sold in boxes carrying labels that claim origin in Chile.

In any event, the public attention that attached itself to that issue has come and gone. The boycott lingers on. But it is out of fashion now. It is time to worry about repression of radicals. It is time to watch the society give up on the effort to encourage racial harmony. It is time to give the covers of the magazines over to the teen-age drug problem, about which nothing rational is being done, just the same howling and the same non-productive outrage. We have utterly forgotten the fashionable unsolved issues of eighteen months or two years ago, like the urban crisis and heart transplants.

For now new cycles begin and there are new issues with which to preoccupy eager minds, massive issues, unprecedented issues that push their way onto the covers of the big magazines by their sheer significance, like the debate over the length of women's skirts.

The phenomena of 'premature abandonment' and of 'inertial life' respond to different kinds of forces affecting, at different times and circumstances, the behavior of ideas in good currency. Both, however, represent deviations from effective public learning. In both, the good currency of an idea depends on factors other than the realities of the situation confronting the social system.

5 Thomas Kuhn's *The Structure of Scientific Revolutions* University of Chicago Press, 1962, presents such a view of scientific discovery in detail.

6 The events which precipitate the emergence of new ideas in good currency may be disruptive to prevailing theory without being disruptive to society as a whole. The 'crisis' may consist, for example, in a technological or economic disequilibrium which presents itself more nearly as an opportunity than as a problem. 'Crisis', then, as I use it here, is shorthand for the emergence of a gap between prevailing theory and reality. It is, in the language of Chapter 2, a situation in which the theoretical dimension of a social system goes into failure.

7 The distinction derives from Raymond Hainer.

8 It is always possible, after an idea has become powerful, to write the history of its precursors. It appears to burst full-blown on public consciousness, but always has an underground history of development in the free areas of society.

9 The point is similar to the one Justice Cardozo makes in *The Nature of the Judicial Process* Yale University Press, 1921, when he points out that laws cannot apply themselves to situations without the development of intermediate interpretive theory.

10 Here, our discussion of the implementation of policy joins our earlier discussion of the devices of dynamic conservatism. For a central government, just as for a corporation, the propose-dispose mechanism may be a way of attempting to limit and contain local innovations in order to maintain the stable state.

11 Among the emergent problems, already visible but not yet of equivalent prominence, are these:

- ◆ The problems of the aged and of disabilities associated with aging
- ◆ Management of the processes by which the decentralization of government, to regional, state, city and neighborhood levels, can be effected
- ◆ Problems and opportunities opened up by bio-medical technology.

12 The fragmentation of existing organizations has its parallel

in the fragmentation of existing policies. Just as adaptive government requires the reintegration of organizations around new problems, so it requires the reintegration of policies. One need only consider, for example, the range of separate and apparently autonomous policies which affect governmental efforts to encourage technological innovation. These include patent, research, manpower, purchasing, loan, tariff and quota, and information dissemination policies, to name a few. Each of these is the responsibility of a separate agency and each has, in general, been designed and administered without reference to its significant impact on technological innovation. Together, these policies represent a kind of keyboard which could be manipulated in the interests of technological innovation. But this manipulation would require, first, recognition of the relevance of these policies to technological innovation and then, development of methods of assessing and taking into account their interrelated consequences.

This would constitute a new technology of policy analysis and manipulation parallel in its effects to the approaches to government organization suggested in the pages that follow.

13 See especially the writings of Warren Bennis, Douglas McGregor, Chrys Argyris.

14 The problem is made more severe by the prevalent myth that invention stops with the first formulation of a program. In fact, as we have suggested earlier, invention continues—often the most critically important invention—throughout the process of implementation.

15 John Macy, former head of the Civil Service Commission, proposed such a plan during the Johnson Administration.

6   Learning systems

1 The secret of mass production and distribution is also the secret of center-periphery government. And numerically controlled production systems, which permit a high degree of product variation along with the economies of mass production, bear a striking analogy to learning alternatives to the center-periphery model.

7   What can we know about social change?

1 Raymond M. Hainer 'Rationalism, Pragmatism and Existentialism' in *The Research Society* Evelyn Glatt and Maynard W. Shelly, eds., Gordon & Breach Inc., 1968, pp. 21–2.

2 Leo Tolstoy *War and Peace* translated by Louise and Aylmer Maude, Oxford University Press, 1941, Book XI, Chapter II, pp. 8–10.

3 There are also economic and political constraints to the design of experiment and demonstration. Consider, for example, the recent fate of the Model Cities Program, which began as 'Demonstration Cities'. Initially there were to be seven cities, then fourteen, then seventy. Because every locality wanted a piece of the pie, no one came up to critical mass. There was, instead, a thin layer of 'equitable' resources for all districts.

Further, there is much in the contemporary political climate —not only on the national scene but in other institutions as well —which militates against experiment. The notion of experiment implies the possibility of failure. And the idea of investing in possible, or even likely failure is anathema to administrations under pressure for successful performance.

4 Several of the issues discussed in this section have been treated at length by Robert Weiss and Martin Rein in their article, 'The Evaluation of Broad Aim Programs: A Cautionary Case and a Model,' in *Annals of the American Academy of Political and Social Science* September 1969, Vol. 385, pp. 133–42.

5 Tolstoy, op. cit., p. 519.

6 The loss of the stable state has a double impact on the experimental model of public inquiry. The first is to render judgments critical to the model inherently uncertain. The second affects the essential social underpinnings of inquiry.

Our concern in the preceding pages has been with public experiment rather than with experiment in the physical sciences. Even here, however, certain features of the experimental process are essentially non-rational and depend upon supports provided by the social system of inquiry. These are, in effect, the non-rational conditions of rational inquiry.

We have had occasion to remark that initial diagnosis of the situation, and of the problem defining the inquiry, depends upon a selection from what is, in effect, a non-innumerable array of information. That process of selection is not subject to experiment since it is itself the condition of experiment; the selection must be made—initially on non-rational grounds—in order to permit the experiment to be formulated and to proceed. Within a social system of inquiry, the inquirer must receive support for his definition of the problem—that is, for his selection. The support of a social system is required, as well, for the movement from the effectively non-innumerable possibilities for experiment or demonstration to *one* design, where the situation provides no rational basis for convergence.

Again, the acceptance of a conclusion as true depends upon our willingness to disregard the aspects of the situation which are incompatible with it—to repress them or to suppress those who are aware of them and would call public attention to them. As William James has pointed out, there is always a periphery of error surrounding any 'conclusion' of scientific theory, and it is only by a form of active common consent that we disregard it.

There is, finally, a form of social support that underlies the whole process of inquiry. Every formulation of hypothesis takes place against a background of stable theory taken as truth. It is impossible, as Peirce said, to question everything at once. And the limited questioning inherent in the experimental model demands active assent to the treatment of residual theory as stable.

These are all among the social conditions of experimental inquiry, without which experimental inquiry cannot take place. But the loss of the stable state undermines the social systems' ability to fulfill these conditions in predictable ways. What the social system of science does for scientific inquiry, the social systems of the larger society do for public inquiry.

The loss of the stable state launches a double attack on the experimental model of public inquiry. It presents the social system with zones of uncertainty for which there is no adequate theory, and it undermines the system's ability to provide support for the non-rational processes essential to experimental inquiry.

7 Hainer, op. cit., p. 20.

◆
◆ Acknowledgments
◆

Thanks are due to the publishers concerned for permission to quote passages from the following works:

The Bond Wheelwright Company in respect of *The Saga of Cape Ann* by Melvin T. Copeland and Elliott C. Rogers; Cambridge University Press in respect of *On Growth and Form* by D'Arcy Thompson and *The Stages of Economic Growth* by W. W. Rostow; Columbia University Press in respect of *Big Science, Little Science* by Derek De Solla Price; Gordon & Breach in respect of *The Research Society* edited by Evelyn Glatt and Maynard W. Shelly; Harper & Row in respect of *The True Believer* by Eric Hoffer; Henry Holt & Co. and Routledge & Kegan Paul Ltd in respect of *Methods of Logic* by W. V. O. Quine; The Macmillan Co. in respect of *Diffusion of Innovations* by Everett Rogers; The Marquette University Press in respect of *Metaphysics and Historicity* by Emil Fackenheim; M.I.T. Press in respect of *Men, Machines and Modern Times* by Elting Morison; Monthly Review Press in respect of *Guerilla Warfare* by Che Guevara (Copyright 1961); W. W. Norton & Co. in respect of *The Wisdom of the Body* by Walter Cannon; Oxford University Press in respect of *War and Peace* by Leo Tolstoy; Tavistock Publications in respect of *The Divided Self* by R .D. Laing; Random House and Victor Gollancz Ltd in respect of *Growing Up Absurd* by Paul Goodman; Yale University Press in respect of *The Dynamics of Culture Change* by Bronislaw Malinowski.